THE ST. ANDREWS SEVEN

*The Finest Flowering of Missionary
Zeal in Scottish History*

THE
ST. ANDREWS
SEVEN

*The Finest Flowering of Missionary
Zeal in Scottish History*

Stuart Piggin & John Roxborogh

St. Andrews

THE BANNER OF TRUTH TRUST

THE BANNER OF TRUTH TRUST
3 Murrayfield Road, Edinburgh EH12 6EL
PO Box 621, Carlisle, Pennsylvania 17013, USA

*

© Stuart Piggin & John Roxborogh 1985
First published 1985
ISBN 0 85151 428 6

*

Set in 10/12 Sabon by
Katerprint Co. Ltd, Oxford
Printed and bound at
The Camelot Press Ltd, Southampton

To
Andrew F. Walls,
Professor of Religious Studies,
King's College,
Aberdeen, Scotland.

Contents

Preface

The St. Andrews Seven is about a university Professor and six of his students. The story of their years together at Scotland's oldest university is a record of the most remarkable flowering of evangelistic and missionary enthusiasm in the history of Scottish Christianity.

The Professor, Thomas Chalmers, was Scotland's greatest modern churchman. Of the 'St. Andrews Six', as we shall designate the students, one, Alexander Duff, achieved lasting fame, and the other five, John Urquhart, John Adam, Robert Nesbit, William Sinclair Mackay and David Ewart well deserve to be remembered.

The 1820s saw a lull in the events of world history, but the birth and growth of Christian vocation within this small group of students in a sleepy corner of Scotland had an impact far beyond its time and place. The way these students met together, prayed and studied, and came to terms with the major challenges to faith in their day remains a pattern for Christian life in universities today.

The mission of the church and personal involvement in it are challenges inherent in commitment to Jesus Christ. In their response to these challenges the St. Andrews Six did justice both to the academic environment in which they were placed and to the biblical faith they had come to share.

First, they aspired to academic excellence. Between them they carried off so many scholarships and prizes that the credibility of their faith could not be assailed on academic grounds: here were students of exceptional ability and industry. From them anti-intellectualism receives no support.

Then they established a student society and ran it with such efficiency and enthusiasm that it quickly became the largest and most successful student society in the University. They were so successful that they provoked a counter-offensive, but they were not wanting in the ability and courage to defend themselves. Not for them the perfunctory performance of those content to maintain a token Christian presence.

Through their society they investigated the missionary call systematically and exhaustively. In this they are a rebuke to those who never get past dabbling with the world-wide mission of the Church. Primarily through close study of the Scriptures they realised that few professing Christians have an adequate conception of the self-sacrifice inherent in Christian discipleship. They maintained that unreadiness for self-sacrifice is evidence, not of the weakness of faith, but of the absence of faith.

But, while they affirmed the necessity of discipline and single-mindedness, they denied that narrowness of outlook had any place. They saw that the Christian should have broad sympathies so that he could relate the Gospel to every sphere of life. They also saw that faith must be personal, but its practice should not be private.

The authors have felt these challenges to their own faith. We are confident that this story of tragedy as well as of achievement, compiled from amazingly detailed records, will speak to all who seek to know and do the will of God in our time.

*   *   *

It is becoming customary for authors to advise their readers on what to expect should they proceed beyond the preface. Chapters 1 and 2 trace the early lives of the St. Andrews Seven. Chapters 3 and 4 recreate student life at St. Andrews in the 1820s and treat some of the intellectual and spiritual problems then facing Christian students. These are perhaps the most unusual chapters in the book and should prove of special interest to university students and their teachers. Chapters 5 and 6 trace the origin and growth of the missionary movement in Scotland in general and at St. Andrews in particular.

In the second half of the book the plot gains momentum and the spiritual temperature rises. The reader is advised to organise his time accordingly: in the first half of the book he should not be disturbed since he will have to concentrate; in the second half, we hope, he will not want to be disturbed!

The interested reader will want to know what happened next and how the 'St. Andrews Six' fitted into the Scottish missionary movement as a whole. The critical reader will want some pointers towards a cool evaluation of the impact of the missionary movement on India. An attempt – all too feeble – is made to meet these needs in the Epilogue.

STUART PIGGIN

JOHN ROXBOROGH

About the Authors

Stuart Piggin is Senior Lecturer in History at the University of Wollongong, Australia, where he lectures in Religious History from the Reformation. He graduated in history at the University of Sydney and in divinity from the Melbourne College of Divinity and received a doctorate from the University of London in 1974. His chief loyalties are to his wife, two daughters, preaching and church growth.

John Roxborogh, a minister of the Presbyterian Church of New Zealand, is at present serving with their mission board as a lecturer in Church History and New Testament at Seminari Theoloji Malaysia, Kuala Lumpur. He is married with four children and has degrees in Engineering and Divinity and a doctorate from Aberdeen.

'Jesus Christ died, the just for the unjust, to bring us unto God. This is a truth, which, when all the world shall receive it, all the world will be renovated.'

THOMAS CHALMERS

Thomas Chalmers, aged 41

I

Chalmers' Grand Design

In November 1823 the most celebrated preacher in Scotland became Professor of Moral Philosophy at the country's oldest University, St. Andrews, thirty miles north-east of Edinburgh. Each needed the other. Thomas Chalmers, aged forty-three, looked for rest from the parish labours in Glasgow which had brought him fame throughout Britain. St. Andrews, with just over 200 students and threatened with a further decline in student numbers, calculated the benefits of acquiring a professor of Chalmers' stature.

In their enthusiasm both parties glossed over the real potential for conflict between them. In a rapidly changing world St. Andrews remained a bastion of conservative 'Moderatism', which emphasised learning and morality rather than doctrine and spirituality. Chalmers, on the other hand, was the brightest star in the new galaxy of Evangelical leaders. To expect the Evangelical Chalmers to live in peaceful co-existence with his Moderate colleagues was asking too much. His arrival was followed by five years of tension and controversy. It also heralded the greatest influx of students at St. Andrews in the nineteenth century.[1] His departure from Glasgow had occasioned dismay and disappointment, the citizens consoling themselves with a civic banquet in his honour, but his arrival at St. Andrews was greeted with unprecedented enthusiasm on all sides. Even the ladies of the town clamoured for admission to his opening lecture only to be told that their presence would be 'unprecedented and unacademic'.

Within a month of his arrival the local press reported:

The popularity of Dr. Chalmers increases daily. The Moral Philosophy class has trebled its members and the prelections are attended by a host of

---

[1] For the 1824/25 Session 420 'regular' students enrolled. A large number of 'irregular' students possibly swelled the numbers to just over 500.

more advanced students and others, to whose accommodation the Reverend Doctor shows every attention. The class met in Dr. Hunter's class-room (the largest in the college) on Tuesday. The old one had previously been crowded to excess.[1]

This was not the first time that Chalmers had been to St. Andrews, nor even the first time he had been a member of the staff. The town had memories of earlier associations to lend colour and contrast to his more recent reputation. In 1791, at the precocious but not unprecedented age of eleven, Chalmers had enrolled in the Arts course at St. Andrews in the United College of St. Salvator and St. Leonard. He then completed the divinity course at St. Mary's Divinity School before leaving St. Andrews and his native Fife (he was born in Anstruther) for further study in chemistry and philosophy at Edinburgh.

The great ambition of his early life was a University Chair in mathematics. This hope seemed destined to fruition in 1802 when he was appointed assistant to the Mathematics Professor at St. Andrews, a position which gave him effective control of the whole course. Chalmers was energetic, talented, opinionated, and tactless. He criticised his professor in public and found himself summarily dismissed. His pride more dented than his self-confidence, he was appointed to the rural parish of Kilmany nine miles west of St. Andrews. To him the chief attraction of Kilmany was its proximity to the University. From Kilmany he maintained a running battle with the Senatus of the University, undermining the enemy through the medium of unofficial lectures in mathematics and chemistry.

Many tales circulated around Fife about this strange young man and his bizarre chemistry experiments. Not surprisingly questions were also raised about the neglect of his parish, especially when it was learned that he had applied for the Chair of Mathematics at the University of Edinburgh. As vigorous in his own defence as he was careless of the Church's welfare, Chalmers maintained that 'after the satisfactory discharge of his parish duties' a minister could 'enjoy five days in the week of uninterrupted leisure for the prosecution of any science which his taste may engage'. Reflecting on this claim twenty years later, Chalmers said, 'What . . . are the objects of mathematical science? Magnitude and the proportions of

[1] *The Dundee, Perth, and Cupar Advertiser*, 27 November 1823.

magnitude. But *then* . . . I had forgotten *two magnitudes*. I thought not of the littleness of time. I recklessly thought not of the greatness of eternity!' Instead he had thought only of his academic reputation. For him personal fulfilment was totally dependent on academic advancement and not at all on the faithful discharge of his pastoral duties as an ordained minister of the Gospel. Without a University Chair, he wrote despairingly in 1805, he was consigned to the status of 'one of those ill-fated beings whom the malignant touch of ordination has condemned to a life of ignorance and obscurity; a being who must bid adieu, it seems, to every flattering anticipation and drivel out the rest of his days in insignificance.'

Chalmers never lost his passionate need to live a life of significance. By 1811, however, he had changed his mind completely about the means by which significance is attained. The process culminating in this dramatic change involved a number of experiences which fashioned him into the most outstanding teacher of prospective missionaries and ministers of the gospel in the nineteenth century.

The beginning of the great change may be traced back to 1806 in which year his brother George died following an illness during which he found comfort in the writings of some contemporary Evangelicals whom Thomas despised. Then in August 1808 his sister Barbara died, and Thomas, who had been commissioned to write the entry on 'Trigonometry' for the *Edinburgh Encyclopaedia* asked if he might also write the entry on 'Christianity', since he now desired to examine its evidences more closely. The death of his favourite uncle, Thomas Ballardie, in June 1809, followed by a serious illness of his own, left Thomas fearful that he would be the next victim. In preparing for what he supposed must be his early death, he concluded that his academic ambitions were insignificant by comparison with the ministerial duties he had neglected hitherto.

His new evaluation of the labours distinctive of the minister of the Gospel was reinforced by his reading Pascal's *Thoughts on Religion*. Of incomparable mathematical genius, Blaise Pascal could nevertheless, as Chalmers observed, 'stop short in the brilliant career of discovery, . . . resign all the splendours of literary reputation, . . . renounce without a sigh all the distinctions which are conferred upon genius, and resolve to devote every talent and every hour to the defence and illustration of the Gospel'. In later years Chalmers was to present to his own students the great challenge of Pascal's example.

The first stage, then, in the process culminating in Chalmers' conversion began, as with many others, in anxiety about his prospects after death. This was followed quickly by his discovery of the strength of the evidences for the Christian faith and the liberating truth that a sense of personal significance need not depend on academic achievement.

The second stage, which lasted through 1810, saw Chalmers struggling to achieve the high standard of personal devotion and dedication to duty which he imposed on himself out of the conviction that salvation consisted of self-preservation through the re-ordering of priorities and the establishment of habits of discipline. In this stage of his conversion process, Chalmers can be compared with John Wesley in his Holy Club days at Oxford and with the early Martin Luther attempting to storm heaven by asceticism. Chalmers' Journal of the period reveals that, as with Wesley and Luther, there was little peace or joy in the struggle as he oscillated between the presumption that he deserved to be saved and despair because his failings suggested that he was far from right with God. He later realised that both the presumption and the despair have one root cause: looking to oneself instead of Christ.

The third and final stage in Chalmers' conversion is best described in his own words, written nine years afterwards in a letter to his brother:

Feb. 14, 1820

My Dear Alexander, – I stated to you that the effect of a very long confinement, about ten years ago, upon myself, was to inspire me with a set of very strenuous resolutions, under which I wrote a Journal, and made many a laborious effort to elevate my practice to the standard of the Divine requirements. During this course, however, I got little satisfaction, and felt no repose. I remember that somewhere about the year 1811 I had Wilberforce's *View*[1] put into my hands, and as I got on in reading it felt myself on the eve of a great revolution in all my opinions about Christianity. I am now most thoroughly of opinion, and it is an opinion founded on experience, that on the system of Do this and live, no peace, and even no true and worthy obedience, can ever be attained. It is, Believe in the Lord Jesus Christ, and thou shalt be saved. When this belief enters

[1] William Wilberforce, *Practical View of the Prevailing Religious Systems of Professed Christians*, 1797.

the heart, joy and confidence enter along with it. The righteousness which we try to work out for ourselves eludes our impotent grasp, and never can a soul arrive at true or permanent rest in the pursuit of this object. The righteousness which, by faith, we put on, secures our acceptance with God, and secures our interest in His promises and gives us a part in those sanctifying influences by which we are enabled to do with aid from on high what we never can do without it. We look to God in a new light – we see Him as a reconciled Father; that love to Him which terror scares away re-enters the heart, and, with a new principle and a new power, we become new creatures in Jesus Christ our Lord.

Now the tales circulating about Chalmers were of a different order. An example may be taken from the pen of Dr. Robert Balfour who visited Kilmany in 1814:

I never saw nor heard him till I came here, but report made him great and good. I went, therefore, to his parish church with very high expectations indeed. They were not disappointed: his talents are of the first order, and now distinguished grace adorns them. He has long been known as a celebrated philosopher and scorner of the peculiar doctrines of Christianity; now, from conviction and with a warm heart, he preaches the faith which once he destroyed. I have had serious conversation with him, and am astonished at a man of such superior powers so modest and humble. He is indeed converted, and like a little child.

Actually, Chalmers disliked such categorical descriptions of his conversion. The minister's role is to proclaim 'the whole counsel of God without partiality', he said, whereas the desire to be thought orthodox often arises from 'the temptation of human praise'.[1] Though he quickly assumed leadership of the Evangelical party in the Church of Scotland, Chalmers proved problematical to his fellow Evangelicals because, while sharing their beliefs, he retained his own inimitable vocabulary.

Yet there was no denying the radical practical changes which resulted from his new understanding of the Gospel. He now preached, not the ineffective moralising sermons of his Moderate days, but 'the utter alienation of the heart in all its desires and affections from God, . . . the free offer of forgiveness through the blood of Christ, and the Holy Spirit given through the channel of Christ's mediatorship to all who asked Him'. Because the Scriptures had now become

[1] W. Hanna, *Memoirs of the Life and Writings of Thomas Chalmers*, Edinburgh, 1850, vol. 1, p. 202.

for him the living Word of God, he set himself to relearn Greek and Hebrew which he had neglected during his student days at St. Andrews. His considerable organising abilities were now devoted to the support of missionary and Bible societies, while insisting that the traditional parish system of the Church of Scotland is the best means of fulfilling the missionary obligations inherent in the Gospel. He set aside the study of mathematics since it could not help him to defend or illustrate the Gospel, whereas he retained his academic interest in economics because he believed it could subserve that end. His views on the areas of academic activity relevant to the defence of the Gospel were not understood by all, but were to influence generations of students.

Chalmers remained at Kilmany until 1815 forging his own synthesis of the best of Evangelical traditions and scholarly habits of thought retained from his Moderate days. Accompanying the new-found concern for prayer, Bible study, personal religion, and the 'peculiar doctrines' of Christianity, which were the distinguishing characteristics of Evangelicals, was a determination, then rare among Evangelicals, to relate this faith to the social and intellectual problems of his day.

In Glasgow, where he served as a minister from 1815 to 1823, his mid-week lectures on business ethics and on science and religion drew such crowds that shops closed as they could not compete with the magnetic orator. He travelled to Edinburgh in 1816 and London in 1817 and took both by storm. Returning to Glasgow, he explored ways in which Christian life could be made possible in a society tottering on the brink of revolution and fragmenting in the face of post-war unemployment and rapid social change. In 1819 he set up the 'St. John's Experiment' in which, with the help of a highly organised and enthusiastic laity, he implemented his ideas on systematic visitation, the use of Sunday schools, and poor relief.

This blend of the spiritual and the practical was the key to Chalmers' appeal. He struggled to release people from what he saw as an endemic fear of *doing* in the Christian life. Such inactivity may have been attributed to a distorted view of predestination, or plain apathy. So Chalmers often spoke of the power of 'pains and prayer' and severely criticised those who emphasised either at the expense of the other.

Chalmers, as we have already observed, also had a rare appreciation of the relevance to theology of other disciplines.

Chalmers saw moral philosophy – provided it concentrated on ethics from which it had been sidetracked by Hume's scepticism – as a handmaid to ministerial training; and political economy (which he also taught at St. Andrews) was in his view a framework for understanding the way society worked, which Christians concerned to apply their faith to the whole of life could not ignore. By accepting a Chair in Moral Philosophy in 1823 and embarking on lectures in political economy, Chalmers, as a key figure in Scottish Evangelicalism, was demonstrating a commitment to holding together facets of the Christian mission which have a tendency to fly apart. Rather than distinguishing between the 'spiritual' and the 'material', Chalmers sought to apply Christian insights to a number of social issues: economics and poor relief, the needs of the working classes, the ethics of the business community, famine relief, and the compatibility of the Christian faith with applied science and technological change. Through the Gospel, then, society is renovated as well as man. This comprehensive vision of 'the Christian good of Scotland', to cite his much quoted phrase, formed the social conscience of a generation of St. Andrews students. Chalmers' refusal to restrict religion to limited areas of human endeavour arose from a deep conviction, derived from his study of the writings of the great American Evangelical theologian of revival, Jonathan Edwards,[1] that truth was a great whole, of which philosophy, science, and revealed religion were inseparable parts. His students quickly caught the vision of their new professor's 'grand design'.

*   *   *

By the 1820s St. Andrews, by-passed by the industrial development then revolutionising Scottish society, was a backwater. Its cathedral, one of the largest in Britain, had been a ruin for more than two centuries; its harbour, once the centre of an opulent textile trade, lay deserted; and in its streets, perpetually swept by east winds, the grass grew undisturbed by traffic. The ancient university, founded in 1412 by Bishop Henry Wardlaw, was in a dilapidated condition. The ancient college buildings, which were so much off the perpendicular that they had to be bound with cross beams, reminded Chalmers of an old cotton mill.

[1] Hanna, *op. cit.*, pp. 16f.

St. Andrews was rich only in the romance of historical association. In the sixteenth century Cardinal Beaton had been hanged
from his castle window, John Knox had preached, and the French
had captured the town. But while the very stones breathed history
they did not cry out, and St. Andrews was easily forgotten by
Edinburgh and even more so by Westminster after 1707 when
Scotland and England were united by the Act of Union. The
university suffered from financial mismanagement and neglect.
Funds intended for building maintenance were used to augment the
salaries of professors. Nepotism was rife in staff appointments, and
although there had been and still were some fine teachers, the main
criterion for appointment was political reliability rather than
academic excellence.

By refusing to take part in corruptions long hallowed by usage,
Chalmers quickly got off-side with his fellow professors. They had
been willing to risk Chalmers' presence among them for the sake of
the new students he was expected to attract, but they were not
prepared to have him rock the boat financially, politically or,
indeed, theologically. By the 1820s Moderatism was ossified at
St. Andrews in its most defensive and anachronistic form. It was
not surprising that the students had voted against Moderatism with
their feet. The professor of logic invariably arrived late for class and
left early as he had written few lectures and had to spin them out.
The professor of church history excelled only in slowness of
utterance: in the University chapel he commenced a sermon on the
text 'Enoch walked with God':

Walking, – my – brethren, – is – that – mode – of – progression – by which
– a – man – by – alternately – advancing – first – one – foot – and then –
the – other, – gradually – proceeds – along – the – road.

Chalmers supplied the missing ingredient – life: enthusiasm and
conviction – and the students returned. The university year or
'session' ran from November through to April the following year.
After the manner of newly appointed lecturers, Chalmers, in
1823/4, prepared his material barely one class ahead of his
students. His lectures were fresh and intoxicating, and as we have
seen, his classroom in the quadrangle of ruins was overcrowded. A
much larger room had to be found, and the following year he
taught the largest moral philosophy class at St. Andrews in the
nineteenth century. The lecture room seated 150, but so many

[8]

crowded in to hear 'the Doctor' that even in the middle of winter, the fire normally essential for warmth had to be extinguished, and the windows thrown open. Students came from England and Wales as well as from the other Scottish universities in Aberdeen, Edinburgh and Glasgow. Some older students who had completed the course re-enrolled to do it again under Chalmers.

Chalmers commenced each class period with a brief prayer followed by a succinct outline of the lecture to follow. In his delivery Chalmers made few concessions to his change from pulpit to lecture room. Some students were so spellbound by the presentation and the vision of comprehensive, systematic, unified truth which Chalmers embodied as well as expounded that they never got past taking down the first sentences. He imparted not just ideas, but a vision – the grand design – taught not just by lecturing, but by inviting participation. Students were interrogated, set prize essays and required to take part in seminars in which they did the major work of presenting each topic. Chalmers' students were not only inspired; they learnt to think for themselves.

The resultant atmosphere was highly conducive to hero-worship. Many of his students were young teenagers, and it is not surprising that someone of Chalmers' strength of personality should have made an enormous imprint on young lives. Of the many who came under his influence we will follow the progress of six in particular. Nesbit, Duff, Mackay and Ewart attended Chalmers' class in his first (1823/24) session, and Urquhart and Adam attended the following year.

John Urquhart was the most brilliant of the six, so that it mattered less that he was one of those generally too transfixed to take notes. Robert Nesbit, more introspective in personality, made a determined effort to write down Chalmers' every word. Alexander Duff was destined to come closest to his mentor in fame, thought and personality, although he imbibed more of Chalmers' elaborate phraseology than his sense of humour. John Adam left his theological studies in Glasgow to sit under Chalmers and, judging by the following reaction, he was not disappointed:

Dr. Chalmers' lectures and even examinations and repetitions are really quite a treat; he has the art of clothing every thing in such vivid colours, his comprehensive mind takes such a grasp of its subject, and his fine imagination and nervous language present such a luminous display of it, as to fix the attention and fill his hearers with delight, whilst he carries them along with him in his new and original elucidations. The most careless are at length fixed in a listening posture, and every countenance bears the mark of the profoundest attention, till his brilliant imagery sometimes irresistibly calls forth the testimony of universal admiration, by ruffing,[1] though forbidden.

We know less of David Ewart and William Sinclair Mackay although Ewart had been attracted by sermons which Chalmers had published on Christianity and astronomy, and Mackay was dependent on Chalmers' patronage and support during and after his time at St. Andrews.

In their first year at St. Andrews students were known as 'bejants' from the French *bec jaune* – signifying the nestling bird gaping for nutriment. It is a good picture of these young men hungry for the vision and inspiration which their hero-professor readily supplied; but it is only part of the story. It would be wrong to underestimate the equally formative influence of their earlier experiences and home backgrounds and the extraordinary effect of their interaction with one another. It was St. Andrews that provided the nest and Chalmers who drew them; but we must begin with an account of their early lives.

[1] Stamping the feet.

'*Few things in the history of religion are more interesting than the commencement and progress of Christianity on a young, an ardent, and a highly cultivated mind. . . . It presents to such an individual a new world, teeming with objects of intense interest, and calling forth his deepest sympathy, and his noblest ambition.*'

WILLIAM ORME (1827)

2

Early Lives

The youngest of the St. Andrews Six, John Urquhart, was born in Perth, twenty-five miles west of St. Andrews, on 7 June 1808. Though a docile child, he was very inquisitive, and it soon became apparent that he was exceptionally intelligent. Sent to school at the age of five, he entertained his fellow-pupils with his fluent reading. Between the ages of eight and thirteen he attended Perth Grammar School and distinguished himself equally in every part of the curriculum. Here he first met Alexander Duff, two years his senior. Together they heard their teacher's dramatic announcement that he would not treat his pupils as animals and that he expected them all to do their duty. Then they watched spellbound as the leather strap or 'tawse' used for discipline was flung into the River Tay.

Duff was always susceptible to the dramatic gesture and never forgot this performance. Urquhart, however, was less excitable in temperament. He had not the same need of the rhetorical and dramatic to arrive at the conclusion that self-sacrifice was life-enhancing. He was precocious, but he did not develop one aspect of his mind or personality at the expense of another. William Orme, his minister in Perth, claimed that he had never met anybody of so fine a mind or who arrived so quickly at maturity.

Orme was a Congregationalist and a staunch supporter of foreign missions, later becoming secretary of the London Missionary Society, an interdenominational body formed in 1795. He was also biographer of the celebrated seventeenth-century Puritan, John Owen, whose works he edited. It was through Orme that Urquhart was directed to the University of St. Andrews. Since he had expressed no desire to be a minister, Orme advised his father not to push him in that direction: uncalled ministers were the curse of the church. But, Orme suggested, at St. Andrews Urquhart would acquire an education suited to any of the professions, including the ministry.

Orme continued to be an important figure in Urquhart's life. In April 1824, near the end of his second session at St. Andrews and six months before he entered Chalmers' moral philosophy class, Urquhart decided to become a full member of the Congregational Church in St. Andrews. He wrote to Orme explaining how shortly before starting university he had committed his life to Christ:

My first impressions of danger, as a sinner, were caused by a sermon you preached on a Lord's day evening . . . At that time, I was very much affected; it was then, I think, that I first really prayed. I retired to my apartment, and with many tears confessed my guilt before God.

Urquhart had delayed joining the Church because he had feared that his 'future conduct' might 'bring disgrace on the religion of the Saviour'. 'But,' he went on to say, 'I have begun to think that this proceeds, in a great measure, from self-confidence, and from not trusting implicitly to the promises of God.' It would have been impressive enough had Urquhart ascribed his reluctance to a desirable self-distrust but, with deeper insight, he saw that his fault was a regrettable self-reliance. Our response to Christ's commands should be determined by what we can do in His strength, not by what we might fail to do in ours. At age fifteen, Urquhart's understanding of his own position displayed a keen spiritual insight.

*   *   *

The most conspicuous characteristic of Alexander Duff was passion. From the cradle to the grave he was passionately high-minded, chivalrous, romantic, and religious. There was a time when he was as passionate a student of the classics as he was of the Bible, but he could never remember a time when he was not a Christian. Born on 25 April 1806 in Moulin in the Highlands of Perthshire, Duff's earliest memories are of the sublime beauty of his environment and the spiritual power of his father. The cottage in which he spent the first eight years of his life stood in an open glade, flanked on two sides by mountain streams and backed by a forest of birch, ash, larch, and oak, which in autumn was a golden spendour. Near-by were the sharp peaks of Ben Vrackie and the unsurpassed scenery of Killiekrankie Pass. His later thought and speech were constituted partly from this physical grandeur and found expression in soaring imagery and lofty sentiments.

Duff's father, James, was a small farmer. He had been converted following the impact on his minister, Alexander Stewart, of the preaching of Charles Simeon of Cambridge, who had unexpectedly visited Moulin in 1796. James superintended a Sunday school and held weekly meetings for prayer and Bible study. Duff was deeply impressed by his father's enraptured prayers and his capacity to reduce his hearers to tears as he dwelt 'on the bleeding, dying love of the Saviour'. When on a stirring theme his speech would rise to impassioned oratory – vibrant, thrilling, indelible. A man of principle, uncompromising and decisive, he realised his son's 'ideal of the ancient martyr or hero of the Covenant'. It is quite impossible to find one quality in the father not replicated in the son.

The religious intensity of Duff's early life and its legacy of high purpose are evidenced by a number of dreams and visions which he experienced. His father fed him from infancy on a strong diet of readings from Foxe's *Book of Martyrs* and Gaelic poetry from the ingenious pen of Dugald Buchanan, known as the John Bunyan of the Highlands. Buchanan had assisted Alexander Stewart to translate the New Testament into Gaelic.

Buchanan's most celebrated poem was *The Day of Judgment*. Its fearful strains so alarmed young Duff that one night he had a terrifying dream where he beheld countless souls summoned before the Judge seated on a great white throne. He watched spellbound as sentence was pronounced on each member of the human race. Panic seized him since he could not determine what would be the outcome of his own trial and he awoke trembling convulsively. Out of this horrifying experience Duff came to an assurance that he was in fact accepted by God through the atoning blood of Christ.

A second experience assumed the same significance in his life as that of the child, John Wesley, who was snatched from an upstairs bedroom of Epworth Rectory, seconds before it was consumed by fire. Wesley believed he was saved for a purpose: 'a brand plucked from the burning'. Duff's narrow escape was from flood, not fire. He was almost drowned in a swollen stream near his home. Shortly afterwards he had a vision of a light far brighter than the sun. From this great light there emerged a golden chariot drawn by fiery horses and from it God Himself called to him, 'Come up hither; I have work for thee to do'.

A third formative experience also resulted from the harsh elements in the Scottish Highlands. In the severe winter of 1819/20, Duff and a companion were overtaken by nightfall when wading through deep snowdrifts en route to Moulin. There was no starlight. They could see nothing. Progress was dangerous, and at one point they felt the ice of a lake cracking beneath their feet. Exhausted, they sat down to rest, praying for deliverance and for the ability to stay awake. Suddenly a bright light flashed on them and then disappeared. They moved in the direction of the light and stumbled on a garden wall. The light was the flare of a salmon poacher and it had been the means of leading them to a cottage where they found food, warmth and safety. In later years when confronted with seemingly hopeless situations, Duff called to mind the flashing light which symbolised for him the over-ruling providence of a loving God.

Perhaps such experiences suggest that Duff was more preoccupied with the experience than the practice of religion. Yet Duff was never morbid or sentimental, nor did he seek such experiences for their own sake, nor commend them as the essence of the Christian faith. His fellow-students at St. Andrews, where he arrived in 1821 having been dux of Perth Grammar School, found him buoyant, energetic, and enthusiastic. He was impulsive but not rash. Here was a man of destiny: with flashing eyes and brushed back hair, his slightly stooped shoulders pointed in the direction he was going as if to emphasise his purposefulness.

* * *

Robert Nesbit was the oldest and the least promising of the St. Andrews Six. He had acute personality problems, indifferent health, and a domineering mother. He was the youngest of eight children and was smothered by his parents, as is suggested by this poem written later in his life:

> I was my father's boast – the centre of
> My mother's tenderest love, and tenderly
> And fully was that love repaid. In her
> All loveliness, and all propriety,
> All beauty, and all excellence, seemed joined.
> The favourite child – the favourite brother, too –
> I was the point where all might meet in peace,
> And entertain one common feeling – love;

I fed on love; and want of love to me
Was want of life.

Nesbit was born in the village of Bowsden, about eight miles south
of Berwick in County Northumberland, on 22 March 1803. His
father, Benjamin, worked a small farm and was an elder in an
English Presbyterian church. From his mother he heard Bible stories
and texts, and, at the age of four, like many of his time, started
'preaching', mimicking the ministers whose sermons he had heard.
Thomas Chalmers himself, aged three, had been discovered in his
nursery, exclaiming in terms laden with pathos, 'O my son,
Absalom! O Absalom, my son, my son!'

By diligence rather than brilliance, Nesbit usually topped his
class at Berwick Grammar School. His chief love was Latin, and in
1816 his ability in classical languages won him a bursary to the
University of St. Andrews. In spite of his age (fourteen) Nesbit, who
was temperamentally retiring and frequently in poor health, never
joined in youthful sports or pranks. He preferred to walk 'inside the
pillars' of the Arts College, St. Salvator's, pulverising his few
companions with argument. He was an inveterate disputant, free
with asperity and sarcasm. His opponents thought him formidable,
but could always console themselves with the view that he was
'prejudiced'.

In 1820, having completed his Arts course, Nesbit entered
St. Mary's, the theological college at St. Andrews, to train for the
ministry. This decision was made on the basis of his academic
competence, irreproachable morals, and punctiliousness in
religious observances. He was unconverted and appallingly self-
righteous. When accused of an offence committed by another,
Nesbit wrote to his mother in the belief that his innocence in this
matter rendered him right with God:

He, indeed, that keeps a clear conscience may advance against the evils of
life with a free and fearless spirit, altogether unknown to the worthless and
profane. . . . Young man, ever preserve thine integrity, and thou shalt never
be moved.

He had yet to discover a better and surer foundation. Early in
1823, the year Chalmers arrived at St. Andrews, Nesbit's brother
was drowned in a storm at sea. Typically, Nesbit's initial response
was to imagine that, if that had happened to him, he would have

been 'safe'. But, whilst reading Jeremy Taylor's *Holy Living*, he was troubled by the thought that he seemed to have no power over his sins. He snapped the book shut, went out, and walked alone, agitated in his quest for a new security. Tears started to his eyes as he realised that through the grace of Jesus, he could count on divine mercy and on the power to renounce every known sin. Yet his was not an over-emotional conversion. He enjoyed no melting happiness as he accepted the full free offer of pardon through faith in a crucified Redeemer. His assurance of forgiveness was never dependent on his own feelings, but on the faithfulness of Jesus.

But there was much more work for grace to do in this narrow, solemn, and unromantic student for the ministry. He was given to censuring what he did not understand, and since his understanding was limited, he was able fully to indulge this propensity. Not surprisingly, he was thought 'illiberal' and 'uncharitable'. He grew up in an area rich in beauty and historical associations, and yet he was quite unmoved by either. He was not a romantic, and there was no way that he would be attracted to missionary enterprise either by love of adventure or by the longings awakened by a lively curiosity. His asperity had to be melted. Zeal had to be created. Perhaps of all the St. Andrews Six, Nesbit best demonstrates that God's grace is perfected in weakness.

*   *   *

John Adam, son of Benjamin Adam, merchant, of Homerton (London), was born on 20 May 1803. As a child he had a strong independent spirit and a tendency to question parental discipline. His education, which ended well, began slowly. He received no regular instruction until he was eleven years old, by which time his reading was still appallingly bad and his spelling atrocious. His father was a deacon in Homerton's Congregational Church whose minister, John Pye Smith, was a 'toff' who wore white gloves in the pulpit. Dr. Smith was a considerable scholar, and tutor at Homerton Theological Academy. Under his preaching Adam, at the age of sixteen, responded to the Gospel, but he later dismissed this response as totally inadequate: 'What I then called repentance was only mortified pride; knowledge was mistaken for faith; excited feeling for love; and external acts for obedience.'

In 1821 Adam became involved in the *Reveille*, a Swiss revival movement of great spiritual depth. At the end of the Napoleonic

Wars in 1815, wealthy Britons were able to resume the custom of touring the Continent of Europe. One such was Robert Haldane, a Scottish landowner, who had been responsible for the rebirth of both the Congregational and Baptist denominations in Scotland. At the beginning of 1817 Haldane began expounding the Epistle to the Romans to university students in Geneva in a series of Bible studies which so contrasted with the rationalist morality then current in Genevan churches that the religious establishment of the city was shaken and the repercussions were felt throughout Europe. Haldane's explosive combination of the biblical doctrine of the Reformation period and intense fervour may be savoured today since his *Commentary on Romans* is still being published.

The *Reveille* was not, of course, exclusively of Scottish inspiration. It fanned the dying embers of Moravian pietism into a new flame. Those who embraced Haldane's views were ejected from the established churches of Geneva and formed three new congregations. The first was the Bourg-de-Four Assembly which had a joint pastorate made up of Emile Guers, Henry Pyt and Henri-Louis Empeytaz. Guers, unable to obtain ordination in Geneva, travelled to London where he was ordained by Congregationalist pastors, including John Pye Smith. Pyt, who also went to London, met John Adam there, and on learning that he was to further his education on the Continent, offered to accompany him to Geneva. Empeytaz was the first to impress Adam with the claims of foreign missions, but Adam, then largely unacquainted with the claims of that work and having an eye for nothing but its dangers, refused to entertain so lunatic a suggestion.

A second congregation was associated with the historian, Merle d'Aubigné, whose writings subsequently had a great impact on British Evangelicalism. The third group gathered around the prominent Calvinist, César Malan, who gave to the Indian missionary movement its most brilliant linguist of the nineteenth century, his son, Salomon. It was to Malan that John Adam went in 1821 to pursue a variety of studies which, his father hoped, might help his undecided son to choose a profession.

Adam was immediately impressed with Malan. His very appearance was 'most apostolical': his hair long, forehead bare, 'and on each side a few little curls'. His faith was fervent, his personality warm, and his manner unusually informal. He addressed his pupils as *chers amis*, began and ended everything with prayer, and his preaching was characterised by 'winning sweetness'. Adam's heart was won immediately. Malan reciprocated. He adjudged Adam the wisest and most diligent of his students and reported finding joy in his company.

Malan's home was surrounded by glorious vistas, and Adam had 'a most delightful view of the lake, the dark Jura, the mountain called Saleve, and the immense range of the Alps stretching beyond, as far as the eye can reach'. But Adam's eye of faith was to behold even more delightful prospects because it was at Geneva that he discerned both the secret of the next life and his vocation for this. Malan emphasised assurance of salvation, and Adam found this a great comfort. He wrote to his father: 'Oh how is this satisfying to the soul to know that the work is finished, that its salvation is accomplished for ever. Oh what peace does it diffuse over the whole man!' He added:

From this change of my views, I have been brought to meditate on my dedication to the work of the Lord; to give up myself, should it be his will, to the sacred ministry, to make known unto others the good news of salvation by a Redeemer. To this end I shall direct all my studies.

Three years before he entered Chalmers' class, then, Adam was a man of direction. At Geneva he studied, frequently for eighteen hours a day, Hebrew, Greek, Latin, French, German, mathematics, music, and drawing, but consistent with his new purpose he concentrated on the study of the Bible. In 1823 he left Geneva and spent a year at Glasgow where he studied Greek, Hebrew, and logic at the University and theology at the Glasgow Theological Academy. The Academy's tutors, Greville Ewing and Ralph Wardlaw, had been profoundly influenced by the work of the Haldanes in Scotland. Wardlaw was destined to contribute more to the cause of missions than any other Scot except perhaps Chalmers himself.

Adam 'loved' Wardlaw 'very much' and it was a sacrifice for him to leave Glasgow for St. Andrews, the more so as it meant relinquishing the hope of obtaining a degree. But sitting at Chalmers' feet was one temptation he could not resist. As he set out for St. Andrews Adam was not to realise that, with his varied and rich educational experience, his maturing aspirations, and his evangelistic zeal, he was himself to prove a catalyst there.

*   *   *

Little is known of the early lives of the remaining two of the St. Andrews Six. David Ewart, son of a tenant farmer, was born in Upper Balloch, Perthshire, in 1806. He entered St. Andrews University in 1821, the same year as Alexander Duff. William Sinclair Mackay was born in Thurso in northern Scotland in 1807. He spent two years at King's College, Aberdeen, which he entered at the age of twelve and where he won high prizes for academic merit. He entered St. Andrews in 1822, the same year as Urquhart. Thus, a year before the arrival of Chalmers, all of the Six had been enrolled at St. Andrews: John Urquhart, precocious in mind and spirit; Alexander Duff, imbued with a potent compound of 'the Gaelic Buchanan and the English Milton, the Celtic fire and the Puritan imagination, feeding on Scripture story and classic culture'; Robert Nesbit, not naturally greatly gifted, but already serious and determined beyond his years; John Adam, already deeply influenced by the fine Evangelical teaching of John Pye Smith in London, César Malan in Geneva, and Ralph Wardlaw in Scotland; David Ewart the archetypal Scot, of strong physique and ruddy complexion; and William Sinclair Mackay, of proven intellectual gifts. There is little doubt that in the St. Andrews Six, their great Professor, Thomas Chalmers, had been given promising material from which to fashion for the Lord's service 'workmen who need not be ashamed'.

'To advance in knowledge is to assimilate the mind to the Omniscient Deity; and though the resemblance can never be complete, it must be increasingly delightful to be ever approximating towards its completion.'

HENRY CRAIK (1825)

3

The Pursuit of
Academic Excellence

In the years 1823 to 1828 Chalmers received many letters from parents, anxious about the future of their sons in the university environment. Fretfully, they envisaged their hitherto well-behaved lads seduced from study and library by the fatal charms of common room and golf course. Such fears were not baseless: many a university student has aspired to no higher purpose than having a good time at the expense of his parents or the ratepayer.

A more subtle enemy of academic attainment, however, is anti-intellectualism which parades in various guises, including religion. In Chalmers' era there were a number of such religious guises. Even in Scotland with its long tradition of scholarship there were those who argued that the only academic knowledge worth having was the 'knowledge of Christ Jesus', whereas the Scriptures (Philippians 3.8) describe that knowledge as 'excellent', not 'exclusive'. There were even some who believed that knowledge was not acquired by patience or pains, but by direct, miraculous illumination from the Holy Spirit. And there were ethnocentric snobs who maintained that prospective missionaries should not waste time in the pursuit of academic learning since they were to labour among ignorant savages.

If a Christian student managed to see through all those guises, he had a further issue to resolve: did academic excellence in itself glorify God, or was God glorified only by useful knowledge?

None of the St. Andrews Six found the temptation simply to have a good time in the least attractive. It is true that, since the fifteenth century, St. Andrews has boasted the world's most famous golf links. It is also true that large claims have been made for the character-building qualities of the game: canniness, strength, resourcefulness, patience, and self-reliance. In his early days at St. Andrews, Chalmers played golf almost daily – surely a conclusive recommendation!

It is significant, however, that Chalmers gave it up on the grounds that 'it weakened his capacity for study'. None of the St. Andrews Six is known to have played golf, or, indeed, any other form of organised sport. Urquhart's chief recreation, for example, was walking: he especially enjoyed exploring the coastline in search of interesting rocks to send to his brother who was dabbling in geology.

Dissipation once reigned at St. Andrews. The famous red undergraduate gown is evidence of that. It was introduced to make students conspicuous, thus discouraging them 'from vageing [wandering about] or vice'. But long before the Chalmers era, sobriety was enthroned at St. Andrews. In 1773 Dr. Johnson visited the town and observed:

St. Andrews seems to be a place eminently adapted to study and education, being situated in a populous, yet a cheap country, and exposing the minds and manners of young men neither to the levity and dissoluteness of a capital city, nor to the gross luxury of commerce.

At the end of his eight years at St. Andrews, Alexander Duff reported, 'There are no gentleman outlaws or privileged desperadoes to gain an infamous notoriety by disturbing the general peace, and setting laws and discipline at open defiance. Billiards and nocturnal riots and other irregularities are . . . unheard of.'

Certainly there was little luxury or privilege in the life of the St. Andrews student and little of the snobbery found in the English universities. Students were then classified as Primars (sons of noblemen), Secondars (the equivalent of Gentleman Commoners at Oxford or Cambridge), and Ternars (those 'of the common rank'). In the fifty years prior to 1820 only two Primars attended St. Andrews, whereas almost three-quarters of students in the 1820s were Ternars. The St. Andrews Six were all Ternars. This circumstance is in itself almost sufficient to explain their conscientiousness, for they were not unmindful of the sacrifice required by their parents to maintain them.

Primarily to relieve the financial burden on their parents, Nesbit, Duff and Urquhart in different years entered for, and won, one of the four bursaries offered each year for matriculants. Urquhart so described this ordeal to his father:

Tuesday was the day appointed for the competition; we met accordingly, at ten o'clock in the morning and got a passage to translate from Latin into English, which we gave in at two o'clock. We were then allowed an hour for dinner, and assembled again at three, when we had another version to turn from English into Latin, which we finished about six o'clock. We were then, without getting out, locked up in a room to wait till we were called in our turn to be examined upon an extempore sentence. I was not called upon till near eleven, when I was dismissed for that night. . . . There were no less than thirty-three competitors, and, as I knew many of them to be very good scholars, from their answers in the public classes, I had given up all hopes of getting one. You may then judge of my very agreeable disappointment, on going last night to know the determination, to hear that I had gained the first bursary.

Urquhart concluded, 'It has certainly greatly relieved my mind as my expenses here will now be comparatively easy'.

The bursaries were valued at £8 per annum for four years, a little over half the expenses of a typical student. Urquhart's records of his expenses at St. Andrews have been lost, but the balance sheets of a near-contemporary, Duncan Dewar, are extant. They show that he spent an average of £15 a year on fees, board and lodging, transport to and from his home in the Highlands, stationery, books, clothing, washing, fuel and lighting.

Students rarely used the run-down college accommodation, preferring private rooms known as 'bunks' for which they paid 4s. a week. In the first session of 1822/23, Urquhart shared his room with Duff thus reducing both his expenses and his homesickness.

There through the long, freezing St. Andrews winter they heated their lodgings with coal, stored under their beds. Lighting was either by tallow candle 'barely sufficient to make the darkness visible' or by a whale oil lamp known as a 'cruisie' which produced more odour than light. They spent less than 6d. a day each on their food: for breakfast, porridge, and, for dinner, broth and a little meat, or bread and milk, or potatoes and herrings. In the evening they usually settled for a cup of tea and had no supper unless invited to a professor's house. In Chalmers' diary we read that he frequently had students to supper, particularly Duff, Urquhart, and Adam. This treat was not without its problems: Urquhart was so lacking in social poise that he found it difficult to cope with

Chalmers' kindness. But, then, the Doctor, as his students called him, was the smothering type.

Clothing was as plain as the food. Even the red gown was not the splendid, long, velvet-yoked Aberdeen cloak it became in 1838, but a rather mean, short, unsleeved garment of medieval design. Jeans, the international uniform of today's university students, were sometimes worn, although moleskin trousers were more common and better suited to the harsh climate.

St. Andrews, it may be concluded safely, produced few gourmets or dandies. But if fleshly indulgence was scarcely a danger to academic attainment, what of mental indolence?

In seeking to reconcile spiritual demands to the pursuit of academic excellence, the Six had a troubled, and therefore experienced, mentor in Chalmers. In addition to lecturing and preaching he was then writing his works on economics. The burden fatigued him, and the fatigue depressed him. He was anxious that through much study he was risking 'secular contamination' and failing both to evangelise his friends and to attend to the spiritual needs of his family. He was so preoccupied with research on economics that he was easily 'soured' by the 'perversities' of his own household: the antics of his six daughters, and especially their untidy bedrooms, maddened him.

It was not that he did not like daughters: on the birth of each of them he would exclaim 'The better article' or 'Another of the best'. It was just that he found them as exuberant as they found him. Even his eldest daughter, Anne, did not behave with the solemnity he would have expected of the eldest daughter. She fell hopelessly in love with Lord Byron, would fall asleep at dinner parties when alone with the ladies and wake up whenever the men came in, and was given to expressing dangerous sentiments like the following:

Last night there was at tea a determined phrenologist. He examined all our heads and told us our characters exactly. . . . He said both Grace and I have too much romance and that there must be nothing but reality! reality! reality! for us. No fiction but all truth. I don't relish that much, because the chief pleasure in life is living in an ideal world and giving yourself up to your imagination.

With such children, Chalmers was brought to realise that the lot of the family man was not an unmixed blessing.

He also wondered if he had made a mistake in coming to

St. Andrews. It was a backwater after Glasgow where he had been such a celebrity. He feared that his academic capacity was ebbing, that his imagination was dimmed, and that he had 'less power of pathos, or fancy, or even intellect'.

Did he have any answers to these tensions and phobias which are occupational hazards for Christian academics? He never achieved his heart's desire of an unbroken sense of communion with God through the long days of study, but these were highly productive years and his public performances in the lecture room and in the pulpit were always effervescent. He coped with depression by confiding, not in his friends, but in his God and his private Journal. He allocated times throughout the day for prayer, a routine he described as 'conforming to an economy of grace, and not of works'. Following prayer for direction in his studies he rationalised his work-load: instead of attempting to master the disciplines of economics and theology together, he would deal with them consecutively, thus reducing pressure and aiding concentration.

In his early life Chalmers had been driven to recklessness by a desperate need to avoid insignificance. Such a personality easily lapses into cynicism when personal ambition is thwarted, but Chalmers never doubted 'the necessity of great and systematic exertion'. He epitomised energetic efficiency. His determination in all circumstances to be effective in the use of time and talents greatly appealed to his idealistic young students. Through 'great and systematic exertion' for Christ they would develop together into 'workmen who need not be ashamed' (2 Timothy 2:15).

Chalmers, then, was a great inspiration to the St. Andrews Six to scale the heights of academic excellence, not for the sake of their own glory, but that they might lay their literary and scientific trophies at the foot of the cross. Chalmers, however, was not the only inspiration. Shortly after his arrival at St. Andrews, Urquhart devoured the writings of two brilliant Cambridge graduates, Henry Martyn and Henry Kirke White. Martyn, chaplain to the East India Company, died in Persia at the age of thirty-one, after a life of self-sacrifice which gave to the Church translations of the New Testament in Hindustani and Persian. White, the Evangelical poet, died at the age of twenty-one, bequeathing 'The Christiad' and other remarkable poems to the infant Romantic Movement.

Martyn, White, Urquhart, and Duff form a succession of Christian scholars who, for the sake of the Gospel, dedicated their considerable talents to the acquisition of knowledge. To be 'endowed with talents', as Urquhart charged his fellow students, was not only 'a matter of high and distinguished privilege'; it was also 'a thing of deep and fearful responsibility'.

If Urquhart believed in the responsible use of academic achievement, he was also aware that it attracted the 'praise of men'. He was led to reflect on this dilemma by the comparison every thoughtful student of the classics makes between the moral values of the Greeks and Romans and those of the Bible. In Greek and Latin there is no word to express humility as a virtue: the love of fame is hailed as a motive to virtuous industry. The Word of God, however, is adamant: 'Seekest thou great things for thyself? Seek them not' (Jeremiah 45:5).

It may be supposed that most zealous, adolescent Christians would reason: 'Here is a clear conflict of values. All human praise must be disclaimed.' Many who so reason react violently, even rudely, to any human praise and trot out the stock response, 'The devil tells me that, too.' It is interesting, therefore, to see what Urquhart thought about human praise and how he responded to it. He had plenty of practice.

His basic insight, remarkable for a seventeen-year-old, was that it was better to control the desire for praise than to seek to destroy it. He wrote:

The love of praise is, perhaps, an original principle of our constitution; and if it be, then it were vain to attempt its annihilation. Nor is this required of us. All that we are bid do in the Bible, is to give it a new direction. And the condemnation of the Pharisees of old, was not that they loved praise, but that they loved the praise of men more than the praise of God.

His classmates, habitually critical of the motives of their fellows, were struck by Urquhart's handling of adulation. One observed:

That Mr. Urquhart was insensible to this praise, would be saying too much. Such an indifference would have proved rather a want of feeling, than an absence of vanity. But whatever secret pleasure he may have felt, it was betrayed by no assumed airs of consequence or pride. . . . No one was forced in his presence upon the disagreeable conviction of his own inferiority so that without any of the arts of pleasing, or those popular qualities that attract general favour, he had made many friends, but no enemies. Few fancied they saw in him a rival to their own ambitious hopes; and when he crossed the path, and gained the hill in advance, it was with so noiseless a step, and with so little show of a triumph, that he either escaped the vigilance of his competitors, or they pardoned his success for the manner in which it was obtained.

The scene at the prize-giving at the end of the 1824/25 session, when Urquhart swept all before him, is described by the same student:

While the more ambitious and showy youths had selected a distant station in the hall, that they might advance to the spot where the prizes were distributed, through a line of admiring spectators, Mr. Urquhart had shrunk unobserved into the corner of a window, near to the seat of the professors, and no sooner was his name announced, than he had again drawn back and disappeared. There was scarce time to put the usual inquiry of who he was, when a new candidate for attention was summoned.

Another fellow student believed that Urquhart was 'totally indifferent to human approbation', attributing this indifference to 'heavenly-mindedness', to 'the perfect liberty of the Christian'. Urquhart seemed unmoved even when, following his reading of an essay to the moral philosophy class, Chalmers himself joined the loud and protracted applause.

Although Urquhart thought it 'vain' to attempt the 'annihilation' of the love of fame, in fact it was evaporating unobserved like water in the sunlight of the love of Christ. Any need of human praise had been dealt a mortal wound. This fact may help to explain why he refused to take his degree of Master of Arts. It must be conceded, however, that many Scottish students then did not trouble to take out a degree.

It was otherwise, but equally curious, with Alexander Duff. He won the prize for the best translation into Latin of Plato's *Apology for Socrates*, and the University Senatus 'spontaneously dubbed him' Master of Arts. Nesbit, through 'exemplary diligence', seems to have won almost as many prizes at St. Andrews as Urquhart and Duff, although unlike them, he was undistinguished in Hebrew, a failure he much regretted later in India when called upon to translate the Scriptures.

John Adam, the product of a more pietistic non-Scottish tradition, and already resolved on entering the ministry, found the appeal of academic life more threatening. At Glasgow he suffered an anxiety felt frequently by the Christian student, namely, that of uselessness when so much needed to be done. Yet he was calmed by the injunction, 'Give attendance to reading ... to doctrine ... meditate upon these things' (1 Timothy 4:13, 15). In his mother he confided:

For myself, I must own I am not ambitious of being what is generally esteemed a learned man, but my prayer is that I may become an able minister of the New Testament. Much rather would I possess the heart-knowledge of the excellent John Newton, than all the head knowledge of the wisest of this world, without it. However, I am aware it may be sanctified, and in that view I am thankful for this valuable opportunity of cultivating it.

At St. Andrews the tension continued as he longed to begin his life's work. 'Though fond of study,' he wrote, 'yet the mathematics, the languages, and even Dr. Chalmers' moral philosophy, seem dry, after the cheering and refreshing labours of the Sabbath ... The sweets of science are not to be compared with those of religion.'

In spite of these reservations no St. Andrews student used his time more economically than Adam. He never indulged in light conversation or reading. Nor could he rest until in studying the Bible 'he could at once recall to memory the corresponding expressions in Greek or Hebrew'. He was a good student and won second prize for an essay on political economy set by Chalmers.

Urquhart, of course, won the first prize.

If, then, the St. Andrews Six grew increasingly indifferent to literary and scientific honours it was not because they were unqualified to excel in them. If they spoke lightly of academic wisdom it was not because they were ignorant of it. If they thought 'secular' knowledge less worthy, they were not disposed to dismiss it as worthless. In turning from the academic to the spiritual they were like mountain climbers who, having scaled what they thought to be the highest summit, found themselves awed, not by the breath-taking view below, but by the discovery of a peak still higher. But the training they received on the first ascent, as they strained towards the summit of academic excellence, was essential discipline for men who were beginning to perceive that their only happiness could be found in a life of 'great and systematic exertion'.

'It is by dint of steady labour – it is by giving enough of application to the work, and having enough of time for the doing of it – it is by regular painstaking and the constant assiduities – it is by these, and not by any process of legerdemain, that we secure the strength and the staple of real excellence.'

THOMAS CHALMERS (1824)

Alexander Duff

4

By Dint of Steady Labour

St. Andrews students in the 1820s received a sound academic training. They were taught the value of taking pains in the collection of data (research), close scrutiny of the data (analysis), and the imaginative integration of findings (synthesis). Particularly in the first and third of these, their mentor, Chalmers, was, yet again, an inspiration.

The indispensable importance of sheer hard work was one of Chalmers' favourite themes, and, indeed, the one on which he waxed most eloquent. In grandiloquent prose which sounds so much better than it reads, he told his students:

... if at all ambitious of a name in scholarship, or what is better far, if ambitious of that wisdom that can devise aright for the service of humanity, it is not by the wildly ... irregular march of a wayward and meteoric spirit that you ever will arrive at it. It is by a slow but surer path – by a fixed devotedness of aim, and the steadfast prosecution of it – by breaking your day into its hours and its seasons, and then by a resolute adherence to them; it is not by the random sallies of him who lives without a purpose and without a plan – it is by the unwearied regularities of him who plies the exercise of a self-appointed round and most strenuously perseveres in them.

One of the most valuable lessons Sir Isaac Newton bequeathed to mankind, Chalmers told his students, was that genius owed her proudest achievements to patience rather than innate talent. While in scholarship, he continued, 'there are higher and lower walks' yet 'still the very highest of all is a walk of labour'. Then, for good measure, Chalmers added the testimony of Dr. Johnson, who when asked if one should await inspiration ('the afflatus') before commencing any writing, replied, 'No, Sir, he should sit down doggedly.' Chalmers was a great exponent of the-one-per-cent inspiration and ninety-nine-per-cent perspiration theory.

In expressing these views, however, Chalmers was preaching to the converted. Urquhart had already adopted regular habits of study before Chalmers arrived. Six weeks after the beginning of his first term in 1822 he described his daily routine to his mother:

Every hour is employed much in the same manner every day. My meals are also strictly measured to the same quantity. I rise every day at seven o'clock, (with candle-light of course), go to the Greek class at eight, and remain there till nine, take my breakfast and go to the library between nine and ten; go to the mathematics from ten to eleven; the Greek again from eleven to twelve; take a walk between twelve and one; go to the Latin from one to two; dine between two and three; study till four; take a walk between four and five; and am in the house the rest of the night: you have thus a history of the time I have spent since I came here.

Not a thrilling history, to be sure, but the regular routine was conducive to hard work. Thrills were to be sought in the realms of the cerebral and spiritual, not in the physical and social.

Once acquired, these habits of constant application were applied as a matter of course to other fields of endeavour. Duff tells how in the university vacation of 1826 he and Adam spent several hours together each day in the 'minute and critical' study of the Scriptures:

Our Biblical apparatus was amply supplied from the University Library, to which we had free and unrestrained access. The best lexicons and critical commentaries were constantly consulted, and the various readings examined and compared.

Nesbit's university career dating back to 1816 had been characterised by the 'constant assiduities', but in the years 1820 to 1823 he took only partial sessions. This academically undesirable custom was entrenched among Scottish Divinity students. At the beginning of each session they merely enrolled and received assignments and then disappeared in search of a teaching position to bring in some money. Chalmers later campaigned against such slackness in the system, and the Evangelical movement certainly revolutionised training for the ministry in the nineteenth century. There may be a connection, therefore, between Nesbit's evangelical conversion experience in 1823 and his decision that same year to complete his

Divinity course with two full sessions, enabling him to concentrate exclusively on his studies. This must remain a conjecture, however, since such a course of action may have been Nesbit's intention all along, and, in any case, Chalmers' coming in 1823 was sufficient to induce him to stay.

A fascinating guide to the diligence of the St. Andrews Six is the record of their borrowings from the University library. In his first session Urquhart told his brother that the library 'is the most important part of the town to me, being no less than my lodgings'. But one searches the Library Receipt Books in vain to find any student who came anywhere near Alexander Duff for the number of borrowings. He took 334 titles (and 413 volumes) home to his 'bunk' during his eight years at St. Andrews. There is no telling how many more books he consulted in the library. We may conclude safely, however, that if, like Wesley, Duff was a man of one book (*homo unius libri*), he brought the insights of many other works to bear on the Bible.

A penchant for fact-gathering stood the St. Andrews Six in good stead when they turned their minds to the consideration of the missionary movement. Their decision to become missionaries was taken only after they had ransacked every available source of information on the subject.

Information has to be evaluated intelligently, however, and here a Scottish university education transcended its English counterpart. In Oxford emphasis was placed on the classics; in Cambridge on mathematics; but in Scotland philosophy was given pride of place. Philosophy taught students to categorise, scrutinise, and criticise data, to ask questions, and to develop judicious interpretations. In short, how to think.

The value of the Scottish emphasis is evident in the case of Robert Nesbit. Though handicapped by slow reading ability and slower comprehension, he nevertheless developed considerable analytical skills. His mind was described as 'accurate, fond of penetrating to principles, and when it had seized an important point, of scrutinising it in every possible relation, so that his application of an old truth often struck his hearers with the force of originality'.

The religious mind is easily attracted by authoritarian argument, particularly the view that because an argument is advanced by respected friends of the cause it must be right. Scottish students were taught to resist this danger. In one of his essays Urquhart declared himself unconvinced by Chalmers' celebrated views on a national establishment of religion. In another he condemned as pointless the distinction made between productive and unproductive labour by economist Adam Smith, although every patriotic Scot was justly proud of this eminent fellow countryman.

Duff's reading also supplies evidence of an enquiring mind. On the one hand, as we would expect, he read the works of such prominent Evangelicals as Hannah More, Charles Simeon, and Thomas Gisborne, and he also consulted those massive, closely argued, unreadable and now unread, defences of orthodox Christianity: Lardner, Leland, Stillingfleet, Conybeare, Waterland, and William Warburton.[1] But, on the other hand, Duff waded at times into waters considered dangerous by many Evangelicals, who were nervous of the impact on young minds of all fiction, romantic poetry, and the writings of infidels.

The first book borrowed by Duff at St. Andrews was a work by the German Romantic, Frederick Schlegel, translated into English just three years earlier. Duff devoured the writings of Wordsworth, Byron, and above all, those of his compatriot, Walter Scott. It can hardly be doubted that the Romantic Movement had a major impact on Duff. He also borrowed the Apocrypha, the Koran, and *The Decline and Fall of the Roman Empire* by the notorious infidel, Edward Gibbon. There was no more convinced Evangelical than Alexander Duff, but his strength of conviction owed much to the fact that he had studied, rather than ignored, 'the wisdom of the Egyptians' (Acts 7·22).

What, after all, were Duff and Adam doing in the Summer of 1826 in their 'minute and critical' study of the Bible? According to Duff they were reviewing the doubts currently expressed about its authenticity and weighing answers made in its defence by apologists. Only after such a thorough and systematic enquiry could they hope to safeguard the deposit of the Gospel (1 Timothy 6·20). Only so could they hope to divide rightly the word of truth, and only so could they be justified in presenting themselves as workmen who need not be ashamed (2 Timothy 2:15).

Another characteristic of the analytical mind is the capacity to communicate clearly, a quality much needed in the preacher of the Gospel. The unanalytical mind substitutes rhetoric for reason. So, it

[1] These six divines were the principal champions of the English Church against Deism.

might appear, does the religious mind. And, it must be conceded, the oratorical skills of Chalmers and Duff were so considerable that in their writings and speeches, the grandiloquent superstructure sometimes obscured the rational foundation.

But Urquhart was different. The chaste elegance of his prose was remarkable. All who heard his essays were amazed by his natural and unaffected style and by his clear, well-constructed argument (the *lucidus ordo*). Only few, however, were aware of the sweat that Urquhart expended in achieving such perfection of expression. Writing essays, it is encouraging to discover, was an irksome, fatiguing task to him, and the only way he ever penned a sentence was by 'sitting down doggedly'.

It was in the realm of synthesis, however, that the greatest intellectual excitement was engendered at St. Andrews during the Chalmers era. Chalmers himself was chiefly responsible because his genius consisted in a capacity to make bold connections, to combine imaginatively previously unrelated areas of thought. That he aimed to cultivate the same capacity in his students is implicit in the title of that essay for which Urquhart and Adam were awarded first and second prize respectively: 'On the mutual influences and affinities that obtain between the moral and economical state of society.' Chalmers was then lecturing in political economy as well as in moral philosophy, but he did not want his students to erect an impenetrable barrier between those two 'sciences'. Similarly, he sought a synthesis between areas of thought, not unrelated, but apparently in conflict, especially science and religion.

Urquhart's prize essay illustrates this integration of philosophy, religion, economics and politics. He argued that economic progress was based on moral improvement. In industrial societies the problem of pauperism has a moral dimension. It is immoral that the working class which produces most of the nation's wealth should be the worst rewarded. Nevertheless, members of the working class, though exploited, would enjoy considerable improvement in their standard of living if only they would husband their limited resources more carefully.

Furthermore, since it is competition among workers which forces down wages, they must not be prevented from combining in trade unions. 'It is absurd to compel an individual, in a country which boasts of its liberties, to sell his labour at a price which can barely supply him with the necessaries of life, and all for the purpose of keeping up the wealth and dignity of his more affluent fellow-countrymen.'

How then was poverty to be remedied in an industrial society? By combination among workers, the amendment of the poor laws, the provision of savings banks to enable the working class to accumulate capital, and religious education for adults in schools of arts and for children in Sabbath schools.

These arguments and the surprisingly mature social conscience displayed owed everything to Chalmers, and illustrate how he involved his students in a search for remedies for the problems created by the social earthquake of the industrial revolution. In the St. Andrews Six Chalmers' synthesis was given international significance, especially in the missionary career of Alexander Duff. Duff was to develop an educational system which integrated literature, science, economics, and Christianity to extraordinary effect. In India Duff's philosophy did not go unchallenged by those who expected missionaries to concentrate exclusively on preaching the Gospel. Even Chalmers was to become anxious that his most celebrated apostle had gone too far along the integration road and wrote warning him to beware of those of 'shrewd, but withal of secular intelligence'. But of those who despised Duff's emphasis on science and economics as 'heathenish innovation', Chalmers condemned their 'weak and drivelling piety' and advised Duff not to heed them.[1]

The St. Andrews Six, then, received a solid academic training in research, analysis, and synthesis. This resulted from a potent compound of the inherited strengths of the Scottish educational system, the vision and example of Chalmers, and the increasingly sanctified ambition of the students themselves. By dint of steady labour, they were now poised for the 'great and systematic exertion' required to elevate Christian students to a position where they would take their place among the key Christian leaders of their generation. The theatre for this exertion was a student society – the highly successful St. Andrews Missionary Association.

---

[1] T. Chalmers, *Posthumous Works*, vol. 6, p. 448.

'There is one thing ... which, by a pious mind engaged in reflecting on the history of the Church of Christ, can neither be overlooked nor misunderstood; we allude to the evident progress which, amidst all ... advances and retrogressions, the course of revealed truth is actually making when considered as a whole.'

MARY DUNCAN (1836)
(her writings were highly valued by Alexander Duff)

5

The Incoming Tide

John Urquhart had a great gift for friendship. He was immensely
popular, and his lodgings the venue of frequent student gatherings.
One autumn evening in the session 1824/25, the session when
Urquhart was to take three first prizes, Duff and a few friends met
at Urquhart's for their favourite activity – earnest conversation.
They discussed the necessity of divine action in the process of
conversion (the work of the Holy Spirit) and the role of human
action (the preaching of the Gospel). They knew that William
Carey, the pioneer Baptist missionary to Bengal, had commented
memorably on both when he said that we should expect great
things of God and attempt great things for Him. Mention of Carey
prompted them to review the policies and successes of missionary
societies.

Then came the momentous question, 'Ought we not also to form a
missionary society?' Some were deterred by the prospect of student
scoffing and professorial displeasure. Urquhart, however, was lyri-
cal in favour of the proposal: Chalmers' support could be counted
on, as could that of a number of their fellow students; if their
society prospered great good would result; if it failed, no harm was
done. Urquhart's arguments prevailed. He quickly produced pen
and paper and urged his friends to draft the plan of a society. Before
they left his room they were to append their signatures. The skilful
advocate had tasted his first victory.

In fact, the society formed by Urquhart was at first confined to
Arts students. A society of Divinity students had been formed in the
previous session probably at the instigation of Robert Nesbit, its
treasurer. On 6 December 1824 the Arts and Divinity societies
amalgamated and the St. Andrews University Missionary Association was born. Within a fortnight it had enrolled forty members,
including John Adam, whom Urquhart met for the first time shortly

before 6 December in the house of a mutual friend who was a member of the Congregational Church. Adam and Urquhart struck up an immediate friendship, and Adam enthusiastically endorsed Urquhart's scheme. By the end of the 1824/25 session membership reached 70 out of a total enrolment of 320 students.

But if this response vindicated Urquhart's optimism, the fears of the faint-hearted were also justified. The infant society was rebuffed in its first act which was to apply to the professors for the use of a room for its meetings. The professors met in the absence of Chalmers and, as anticipated, there were many frowns. They muttered about the 'thoroughly unacademical' purpose of the new society. Such a 'Puritanical and Methodistical' organisation would divert students from their proper studies. The application was 'politely though peremptorily negatived', and the refusal was accompanied with the recommendation that such permission 'ought only to be granted when the objects of the Society were literary or scientific'. As a result, the students had to settle for a tiny, dark, and inconvenient private school-house in a dingy part of the town. This set-back helped to convince them that they were a persecuted minority, and could expect nothing but opposition from those who, as Duff said, 'still creep in the dust, and grope amid the fogs of an earthly atmosphere'.

Despite their awareness of other societies, which had encouraged them to form their own, the Evangelical students at St. Andrews underestimated the strength of the emerging missionary movement. A well-informed international and historical perspective on the movement was needed to dispel this impression of weakness. Such a perspective, which the students were soon to acquire through their society, showed that, in the first place, student societies akin to theirs were being formed all over the Evangelical world, and, secondly, missions had come of age in Scotland.

Similar associations had been formed in Aberdeen in 1820 and in Glasgow in 1821. In 1825 a student missionary society was formed in Edinburgh at the behest of Nesbit's friend, John Wilson, destined for a great missionary career in Bombay. The St. Andrews students eagerly corresponded with all these associations. They also exchanged letters with a society formed in Belfast in 1826 and with the Andover Seminary Society of Enquiry which had been formed in America in 1811, to challenge every divinity student with the possibility of foreign missionary service. The flood-tide of missionary enthusiasm had reached the universities.

Admittedly the tide had taken many centuries to reach the level where it overflowed the barriers erected against it. Missionary endeavour in Scotland may be traced back as far as Ninian in the fifth century A.D., Columba in the sixth, and Kentigern in the seventh, although they were more often venerated as saints than emulated as missionaries. The Scottish Reformation was of missionary potential if not achievement: the Scots Confession of 1560 carried in its title page the text of Matthew 24:14, 'And this glaid tydingis of the Kyngdome sall be precheit through the haill warld for a witnes unto all natiouns, and then sall the end cum.' The 1645 *Directory of Public Worship* stated that ministers should pray 'for the propagation of the gospel and kingdom of Christ to all nations'. At the end of the seventeenth century, the Church of Scotland General Assembly instructed the six ministers who sailed with the settlers in the illfated Darien Scheme to propagate 'the glorious light of the gospel . . . among the nations for their instruction and conversion'. Early in the eighteenth century the Society in Scotland for Propagating Religious Knowledge was founded with the object of 'promoting Christian knowledge and increase of piety and virtue within Scotland . . . and for propagating the same in popish and infidel parts of the world'. One of its missionaries was David Brainerd, whose short, consecrated life among the North American Indians was as much an inspiration to the St. Andrews Six as that of Henry Martyn in another sphere of service.

The missionary momentum was quickened in the Scottish Revival beginning at Cambuslang in 1742. Out of this grew the 'Concert of Prayer', an ongoing commitment by some Scottish ministers to unite for prayer to 'revive true religion in all parts of Christendom and fill the whole earth with His glory'. The Concert of Prayer directly influenced the founders both of the Baptist Missionary Society in 1792 and of the London Missionary Society in 1795. In February, 1796, the Glasgow Missionary Society and the Edinburgh (later Scottish) Missionary Society were formed.

In the same year the General Assembly rejected a motion to authorise a general collection throughout the Churches in aid of missionary societies. A far more significant step was taken in 1824 when the General Assembly agreed to establish a network of

Christian schools in India. Few at St. Andrews realised the revolutionary implications of this decision. The Church of Scotland was now itself part of the missionary movement. The incoming tide had breached the last barrier.

At St. Andrews the missionary revolution was led by Thomas Chalmers. For many years he had been in great demand as a speaker at missionary rallies. The first indication of his interest in foreign missions is found in his Journal for August 1811 where he noted that he was 'much impressed by the work and utility' of the Baptist Missionary Society in India headed by William Carey. 1811 was also the year of Chalmers' conversion, suggesting that the missionary impulse was the natural reflex of his God-given faith. Chalmers himself insisted that the desire to evangelise grew out of the reality of evangelical experience:

Those to whom Christ is precious, will long that others should taste of that preciousness. Those who have buried all their anxieties and all their terrors in the sufficiency of the atonement, will long that the knowledge of a remedy so effectual should be carried around the globe.

Opposition to foreign missions stemmed from those who had not experienced the effectiveness of the remedy and who were reluctant to commit the Church of Scotland to the revolutionary changes ushered in by the new missionary movement. But if those were the real reasons, Chalmers found himself confronted with a number of ostensible objections – philosophical, theological, and economic. To those objections, Chalmers, by 1823 widely read in missionary intelligence, had developed a formidable missionary apologetic.

To the philosophical argument that the heathen must be civilised before they could be Christianised, Chalmers replied that it was 'both doctrinally and experimentally untrue that a preparatory civilisation is necessary ere the human mind can be in a state of readiness for the reception of the gospel of Jesus Christ'. It was not that Chalmers doubted that, in practice, civilising frequently accompanied conversion, but he insisted on maintaining the possibility that the two might be divorced, since the obligation to believe the gospel belongs to every person by virtue of his humanity rather than his refinement.

The theological argument that the doctrine of election meant that it was not necessary to offer the Gospel freely to all men, Chalmers dismissed as 'unintelligent'. The 'unexpected amnesty' found at the heart of the Gospel is to be 'held forth to every creature under heaven', he insisted. And on the evening before his death in 1847 he returned to this point: 'In the offer of the Gospel we must make no limitation whatever' because 'God commandeth *all men, everywhere* to repent'.

A third common objection was the economic one that missions deprived the home churches of scarce resources. Charity begins at home. But Chalmers replied that it did not end there, and that, in any case, involvement in foreign missions had many reflex advantages for the sending churches. One such advantage was a stronger financial position since giving worked according to a 'fermentation' rather than an 'exhaustion' process: giving in one area encouraged giving in another.

The difficulty at St. Andrews was to find a platform to give this ripe exponent of missions full opportunity to champion the cause. The student society was not that platform since Chalmers well understood that student societies are best run by students. A town missionary society had been formed by the Independent pastor, William Lothian, and others in 1822, but the university professors were unimpressed. In December 1824, shortly after the formation of the student society, Chalmers was invited to become President of the town society. He diplomatically declined until more senior professors had been approached first. Robert Haldane, Principal of St. Mary's Divinity Hall,[1] not only declined the invitation, but also refused to allow the society to use the town church for the annual sermon.

Haldane and the Church History Professor, George Buist, were rumoured to be 'inimical to public meetings', whereas Chalmers, after his success at Glasgow, was known to be convinced of their utility.

Chalmers, therefore, entered into his rightful inheritance. He presided over the town association for the first time on 7 February 1825. The students were present, having resolved earlier to shorten their own missionary meeting so that they might hear their beloved doctor in full flight. They were not disappointed as they witnessed Chalmers take the chair and 'in an impressive speech advocate the cause of missions and recommend unity and zeal'.

Urquhart was particularly thrilled with 'the perfect originality' of

[1] Not the Robert Haldane (Commentator on Romans) previously mentioned.

Chalmers' procedure. 'Dr. Chalmers,' he wrote, 'is, in the widest sense of the word, a Philosopher; and philosophy is his companion wherever he goes . . . He seems to regard the history of Christian enterprise among the heathen, as a wide field of observation, from whence he may gather, by induction, some very important truths in reference to the Christian religion.' Urquhart refers here to Chalmers' habit of ransacking missionary registers and books for interesting data from which he drew generalisations which not only applied to the missionary movement as a whole, but which also provided further evidence for the truth of the Christian religion.

Chalmers explained, always sympathetically, the policies and philosophies of a large number of missionary societies of different denominations. This was but one manifestation of his large-minded tolerance. He also pleaded against attempts to force Irish Catholics to become Protestants by civil penalties. Force, he argued, rivets the chains of superstition. The only legitimate and effective instruments of conversion were Scripture distribution, education, and preaching. Similarly 'with his usual felicity of illustration and argument', he combated the prejudices of those who opposed the education of the working classes and the heathen on the grounds that it made them seditious.

Chalmers also attracted to St. Andrews some of the most celebrated missionaries of his age. Joshua Marshman, of the Baptist Missionary Society, spoke of the college, opened at Serampore in 1818 for native missionaries and educated Hindus. Robert Morrison, of the London Missionary Society, reported on his labours in China, of his Chinese dictionary and Bible translation, and of the 10,000 Chinese manuscripts he had procured through eighteen years' work in China. Henry Townley, also of the London Missionary Society, spoke of a young Brahmin who had become his fellow labourer and of the Indian village where a Christian church had been constructed from stones previously used in a Hindu temple, while John Curruthers, of the Scottish Missionary Society, tantalised his hearers with stories of his exotic adventures in Russia.

The benefit of all this to the students was incalculable. They imbibed Chalmers' theories and breadth of vision. They learned from the experiences of missionaries themselves. And sometimes they were permitted to practise pleading the missionary cause from the platform Chalmers had made so popular. Duff was the most prominent of the student advocates as, with Chalmers' florid vocabulary, he forcibly 'illustrated the adaptation of the Gospel Scheme to the moral condition of man'.

Nesbit reported that Chalmers now swept all before him. Large numbers attended the meetings, and even Haldane and Buist could not forgo meeting visiting missionaries who were among the finest linguists of their day. Indeed, professorial opposition to the missionary societies was beginning to evaporate. These gratifying results are attributable not only to Chalmers' innate genius. He sowed more prayer and pains in the fertile soil of the St. Andrews Missionary Society than in any activity apart from his professorship. And he reaped in joy. At his last meeting as President in 1828, as he acknowledged the thanks lavished upon him, he seemed 'to labour under considerable embarrassment from the intensity of his feelings'.

Not the least of his society's achievements was its contribution to the missionary training of the St. Andrews Six.

'Well can I trace the dawn, the rise, and progress of any feeble Missionary spirit I possess, to the readings, conversations, and essays called for by the student Missionary Association in St. Andrews.'

ALEXANDER DUFF (1831)

6

A Well-run Student Society

When Duff, Urquhart, Adam and Nesbit formed the St. Andrews University Missionary Association in 1824, they were without the international and historical perspectives reviewed in the previous chapter. They were unaware that students all over the Evangelical world were uniting for similar purposes. Nor did they perceive that the incoming tide of missionary zeal, for so long latent in Scottish Christianity, was about to burst the banks of traditional opposition. And Chalmers' great work with the town association lay in the future.

Without these encouragements, the students rested their hopes for a remedy to evangelistic inactivity in a well-run organisation among themselves to foster missionary zeal. This necessitated the formulation of clear aims, a just and workable constitution, and a procedure for regular and interesting meetings.

Urquhart's conscious aim was to stimulate interest in and commitment to missions and to emulate at St. Andrews the missionary spirit which in the previous generation had descended on Simeon's Cambridge and sent the chaplains Henry Martyn, Claudius Buchanan, and David Brown to Calcutta.

The society's aims were expressed in its title: 'An Association among the students of the University of St. Andrews for the Review and Support of Missions.' The review of missions was given priority. As Urquhart explained, 'the great object we have in view is to obtain and circulate missionary intelligence among the students'. Accordingly, it was resolved at the very first meeting on 6 December 1824 to establish a library 'consisting of the periodical publications of Missionary Societies and other books connected with missions'. At first the society spent most of its funds buying the biographies and writings of missionaries, for, reasoned Urquhart, 'we are sure that there are few who can peruse the diary of a Brainerd or a

Martyn without being animated with something of their devoted spirit'.

Duff, who, it will be remembered, had an insatiable appetite for reading, was soon appointed librarian. His task was not only to catalogue the society's books and keep them in a cabinet which the students purchased for the purpose, but to distribute the books, and see that they were circulated. In Duff's hands nothing would collect dust, particularly books.

Urquhart was not so optimistic about the second aim, which was to raise money to support other societies. 'We do not expect very large contributions,' he wrote, 'and the assistance which we can render to the cause may be, comparatively, but trifling.' Nevertheless, as an annual membership fee, each student member contributed 3s., the equivalent of three quarters of a week's rent. As their membership was 70 to 80 for each of the sessions 1824/25 to 1828/29 and as the students augmented their funds by collecting from the well-disposed, they were able each year to send worthwhile sums to the larger missionary societies. For instance, in 1826 they voted a sum of £3 to the Scottish Missionary Society, and £2 each to the Baptist Missionary Society, London Missionary Society, the Continental Society, the Hibernian Schools Society, and the Gaelic Schools Society.

The student missionary society was an amalgamation of Urquhart's society of Arts students with Nesbit's society of Divinity students and the constitution adopted was rather complex – in itself evidence of the high seriousness with which the students viewed their task. Robert Nesbit, treasurer of the Divinity society, solemnly laid the Terms of Union before the Arts society from the United College. There were to be two Presidents, one from each college, and four Vice-Presidents, two from each college. The Secretary was to be elected from the Divinity students, and the Treasurer from the Arts students. Each session was to commence with an address by the Divinity President and conclude with an address by the Arts President.

Of fourteen committee members elected at the first meeting, four were of the St. Andrews Six. Duff was a Vice-President; Nesbit, Secretary; Adam, Treasurer; and Urquhart, a member of the committee. Despite his leading role in the establishment of the society, Urquhart, always conscious of his youth, would consent to serve only as a committee member. Other committee members included

William Scott Moncrieff who, on his arrival at St. Andrews, had been commended as a shy lad to Chalmers' protection by an anxious parent but who was to prove himself a person of courage and good humour, and William Tait, who was to become an Anglican clergyman after a time in the Catholic Apostolic Church. Moncrieff and Tait were close friends of the St. Andrews Six, as was Henry Craik, who became a member at the second meeting of the missionary society in January 1825, and who was destined to join the Brethren and do a life's work at Bristol in harness with George Müller, the celebrated philanthropist.

The society was to meet on the first Monday of each month at 5 p.m. One or two essays written by members and extracts from missionary journals were to be read at each meeting. Criticism of essays was not encouraged and debates on controversial issues were disallowed. Accumulating data, fostering missionary zeal, and challenging every member with the question of his personal responsibility for engagement in the missionary task were considered more important than the metaphysical wrangles which were the traditional fare of Scottish student societies.

Missions apart, the society became the chief means by which the deeply committed explored the implications of Christianity for their lives as University students. Henry Craik read an essay on 'The legitimate effects of the association on its members'. The society, he said, enabled students who were 'willing to speak on the subject of religion' to get to know each other intimately, and it 'demanded imperiously and was well calculated to secure' a daily study of the Scriptures which it was a purpose of the society to disseminate. Daw, another student, read a 'very interesting and highly intellectual essay' on the 'Evils of the Academic Life and the way in which this society may be disposed to remedy them'.

The essays which Adam and Urquhart read to the society have survived. They are original, well-informed and closely argued. Adam's first essay, though written in the busy term while he attended Chalmers' lectures and wrote his prize moral philosophy essay, was based on impressive research. For this essay he read Brown's *History of Missions*, Crantz's *History of Greenland* with special reference to the Moravian mission, Mrs. Judson's *Letters* on the mission to Burma, Buchanan's *Christian Researches in Asia*, which was a study of India, and 'Hope', an epic poem on the Moravian mission in Greenland by the Evangelical poet, Cowper.

On reading these works, Adam was amazed at the success which attended the preaching of the Gospel in the previous generation. He concluded that this work was of God and compared favourably with 'the success which attended the first preaching of the Apostles in the age of miracles'.

So, in his essay to the society, Adam, by an appeal to facts, as well as by theological argument, answered those who branded 'every missionary attempt as chimerical and absurd'. No one was more influenced by this essay than Adam himself. Hitherto he had thought only in terms of the home ministry, and it was while he prepared this essay that he began to wonder if he was inconsistent in exhorting others to become missionaries and yet shrink from the work himself. From this point, and for the first time, Adam's letters refer repeatedly to the subject of foreign missions.

Urquhart did not read his first essay until a deferred meeting of 12 February 1825. It was an exhilarating time for 'the lad' as he was now known. Chalmers' lectures on moral philsophy and on political economy were expanding his horizons daily. He was also fully involved in a number of student societies. On 11 December 1824 he had read to the Literary Society a paper entitled 'That Knowledge gives its Possessor more Power than Wealth does'. On 10 February 1825, just two days before his paper to the missionary society, he had preached for the first time. His sermon was heard by a few fellow students who had formed a society for extempore preaching.

Yet a shadow had fallen across Urquhart's path. Early in January 1825 he was called away from the Doctor's classes and student activities to Perth to the bedside of his brother, Henry, who was seriously ill. Urquhart was distressed to find his youngest brother in 'excruciating' agony, 'violently crying out from the pain in his head'. In that condition he died. The experience was salutary. For the first time Urquhart was forced to think through the reality of death, a process prolonged by the fact that his brother took some weeks to die. At his bedside and by letter, Urquhart had encouraged him to trust Christ to carry him safely across the valley of death.

Back at St. Andrews, Urquhart deliberately 'overburdened' himself with 'business'. He poured out his soul in a long letter to his old adviser, William Orme. 'The wound is yet green,' he wrote. The fact that he was in mourning probably accounts for the subject matter and solemnity of his essay to the missionary society entitled

'The Doctrine of a Gradation in Rewards and Punishments and an attempt to apply it to the Subject of Missions'.

Urquhart accepted a fundamental, if unpopular, premise of Evangelical preaching, namely, that there are only two classes of men, the children of grace and the children of wrath (Ephesians 2:1–6). The distinction is plain in the New Testament (for example, Matthew 13 and 25), but on the basis of such passages as Luke 19:12–27 and 1 Corinthians 3:10–15, he argued that on the one side of this divide there are different degrees of glory, and on the other, different degrees of punishment. If in the early Church those who sought a high reward in heaven identified with Christ in the sufferings of martyrdom, so it is open to Christians today to identify with Him in his capacity, not as a martyr, but as a missionary. The missionary stood to win the brightest crown:

There is such a thing as being saved, yet so as by fire; such a thing as being least in the kingdom of heaven. And even this is a thought of highest ecstasy; but there is a thought more ecstatic still. It is the thought of an abundant entrance, and an exceeding great reward, and a crown of glory that fadeth not away, and a splendour like the shining of the stars in the firmament.

Urquhart also confronted his hearers with the serious consequences of failing to use talents (including academic powers) for the glory of God.

Mental endowments are gifts, which, more than any other, perhaps, have been alienated from the service of Him who gave them. And it will not be the [least] condemnation of by far the greater part of those who have received them, that they have wrapt them in a napkin or buried them in the ground. Not only have they been withdrawn from the service of God; but far too frequently they have been employed in the service of his enemies.

Urquhart rejected the prejudice of those who refused missionary service on the grounds that they were over-qualified. 'We know no office in the Church of God,' maintained Urquhart, 'where the very highest mental attainments can be more beneficially employed, than in the office, all despised as it is, of the Christian missionary.' He concluded by answering the objection that a concern for heavenly reward is basically selfish. With psychological shrewdness, Urquhart observed that heavenly reward is only an issue for those who are first constrained by the love of Christ themselves to live 'not unto themselves'. But once motivated by the love of Christ, the added inducement of heavenly reward would be a defence against sloth and sentimentality.

Urquhart's familiarity with the Scriptures and the ease with which he reasoned from them marked him out as a keen and intelligent Bible student. The subject of his essay was difficult and fraught with problems. Yet he dealt with objections systematically while avoiding the impression that he was engaged in a mere intellectual exercise. The object of the missionary society, he believed, was 'the most important which can engage the mind of a Christian'. Evidently Urquhart was concentrating increasingly on this one issue.

The 1824/25 session ended on an auspicious note for the infant missionary movement at St. Andrews. Chalmers was now safely in possession of the town association. Seventy members had joined the student society. The Principals of both the United and Divinity Colleges had at length accepted the invitation to act as patrons of the society, a change of attitude viewed as almost miraculous by the students. And the society was blessed with outstanding members. Regrettably 1824/25 was the last session Robert Nesbit spent at St. Andrews, but he was known to be investigating the possibility of overseas service, and while with him the society lost an indefatigable secretary, he was replaced by the able zealot, Henry Craik. Duff, an irrepressible enthusiast, was about to commence his Divinity studies: no doubt he would make his influence felt at the Divinity College. John Adam and John Urquhart would enter their final year in the philosophy course. Adam was by now an experienced evangelist, and Urquhart was fast developing into an irrefutable apologist for the missionary cause.

In high excitement the students anticipated the 1825/26 session. Perhaps it would be the year of wonders.

'Why, the whole fun of the thing lies in your being but a set of boys . . . you have put away . . . the buoyancy of boyhood . . . by aiming at the lofty, you have achieved only the dull.'

GILBERTON GARRULOUS,
St. Andrews University Magazine,
14 January 1826

7

Student Politics in the Year of Conflict

19 November 1825 was a hard day for William Scott Moncrieff. He was by nature timid, but, like Adam, he had studied at Geneva under Malan, and had there acquired courage. So, on this day, he stunned members of the missionary society gathered for their first meeting of the 1825/26 session with a blistering attack on 'the pernicious folly of those who persist in pouring forth their sarcasms on men who are engaged in an employment so sacred and so glorious as that of a Christian missionary'.

Then he returned to his garret study and collapsed in his easy chair, a gift from his grandmother, and stared into the fire. His mind was fixed on one question: What else could he do to further the missionary cause? Craik called to congratulate him on his 'forceful' and 'feeling' paper, but in spite of the characteristic flamboyance of his entrance, Moncrieff barely noticed him.

Moncrieff's landlady chided the host for his lack of hospitality and fussed with her best china, preparing tea. She was handicapped by loneliness and deafness, and as she strained the tea she also strained her ears to overhear the lads' conversation.

Suddenly, the preoccupied Moncrieff exclaimed, 'I think I'll set up a periodical.'

His landlady was appalled. 'Set up to be a prodigal, Maister William,' she said, 'and break your mither's heart, na, na, I winna let you do that, my man.'

She could not easily be calmed, so Moncrieff and Craik deserted the garret, and hastened to William Tait's lodgings, collecting prospective contributors on the way. The entire party was seized with mania. Tait was mocked mercilessly when he attempted to cool

proceedings by taking an age to calculate the quantity of tea proper
for such a large gathering of prospective journalists.

On the basis of ancient prejudice they declared that females could
not understand mathematics, and as the magazine had to please
them, no fluxions or conic sections would be admitted. No comic
sections would be admitted either, as punning might degrade the
project. Genuine humour would be admitted, as would plenty of
religion and mature reflexions on the arts and sciences, and it was
hoped that there would be enough 'scented silk handkerchief
gentlemen' about the University to write pretty sentiments which
might be passed off as poetry.

So, on 3 December 1825 the *St. Andrews University Magazine*
was launched, edited by one 'Tari', since Moncrieff, Craik, and
Tait, out of custom rather than fear, preferred anonymity.

This good-natured production met with a hostile reception since
it appeared right in the middle of a student revolution. For the first
time in living memory the students were consumed with interest in
the election of a new Rector for their University. Like Duff, most of
them were addicted to the writings of Sir Walter Scott, and they
determined to make him Rector. But Sir Walter was not eligible.
The candidate had to be one of only four persons, the two college
Principals and the Professors of Divinity and Church History, a
respectable but dreary lot by comparison with the national bard.

The students persisted in nominating only Sir Walter, an act
tantamount to revolution, for it involved ignoring the University
statutes and defying the Senatus. The student leaders were
threatened with expulsion and, since most of them were in training
for the ministry, their future careers were jeopardised as no Presbytery would admit an expelled student.

The matter stood quite unresolved, and the tension was
unabated, when the 'Tari' announced the advent of a student
magazine. A section of the students immediately suspected a con-
spiracy. The professors, they declared, had bribed meek, religious
students to bring out a tame magazine to displace the *Argus*, a
student magazine laced with more traditional revolutionary student
fare, namely, 'insolent aspersion' and 'obscure jocularity'.

It was a ridiculous charge. True, the two Principals now patron-
ised the missionary society, but not with any enthusiasm. Theirs
was hardly an endorsement of Constantinian significance!

The editors, however, were more concerned to deny the aspersion on their manliness than that on their professors' integrity. 'We yield to none in the independence of our sentiments,' they declared, '. . . and in undisguised abhorrence of anything like cringing and temporising policy.'

By now the Evangelical students were skilled in the language, if not the art, of disputation, and they used their magazine to repay their opponents in kind. To those students who decreed that all 'veneration of religion' should be eliminated from university magazines, William Tait asserted that this decree was prompted by 'the universal tendency of man to magnify what is truly insignificant, and depreciate what is truly great'. To opponents who accused them of religious bigotry, he declared, 'It is our firm determination to hold by the opinions deemed Evangelical at whatever risk.' And to those students who prophesied, quite rightly in the event, that the magazine would soon collapse as it was the work of only 'a few boys', the youthful editor replied, 'If we do not show by the spirit and strain and style of our writing, that we are more than a few boys, our opponents may glory over us.'

Two days later, on 5 December 1825, the besieged students held their monthly missionary meeting. They elected their two best men to the dual Presidency, Duff, as Divinity President, and Urquhart as Arts President. Adam retained the Treasurer's post. Duff then read an essay 'ingeniously' refuting the usual objections made to missions. Craik, who was re-elected Secretary, recorded enthusiastically, 'With a high degree of energy and imaginative beauty this Essay appeared to combine an uncommon portion of original reflection and ingenious argument.'

But not all students were so enamoured of Duff. While he was delivering his paper to the missionary society, a more venerable student club, the Theological Society, was deliberating on the application for membership of this new Divinity student. The Theological Society was open only to Divinity students and it jealously scrutinised every applicant for membership. This Society appears to have become the chief venue for rivalry between the students who supported the Moderate party in the Church of Scotland and those who supported the Evangelical party, known as the 'High-Flyers'. Robert Nesbit and William Sinclair Mackay had in earlier sessions both gained admission to the Society, and Nesbit had been elected Secretary on 7 January 1824, a few weeks before he became Treasurer of the newly-formed missionary society among the Divinity students. He introduced for discussion at meetings of the Theological Society topics of interest to the missionary-minded. For example, on 20 March 1824, he spoke so long in support of Bible societies that, as he himself recorded in the minutes, the members were greatly annoyed. When the customary vote was taken after his address, six members voted in favour of Bible societies and seven against.

A further indication of antipathy to Evangelicalism came in the next session (1824/25) when Henry Craik, who had just become a Divinity student, was twice proposed for membership and twice refused. In fact, he was never admitted to the Theological Society.

To return to 5 December 1825 – Alexander Duff and Donald Stewart were both proposed as members. Stewart was a well-known Moderate and he was elected unanimously. The arch-Evangelical and newly-elected President of the missionary society, however, was elected only by a narrow margin. In subsequent elections William Tait also just made it, while David Rintoul, also prominent in the missionary society, was thrice nominated and twice rejected.

Duff proceeded inexorably to take over the Theological Society as he did the missionary society. He was quite irrepressible, never conceding that there was any virtue in strategic retreats. The first meeting of the Theological Society which he attended was on 10 December 1825, a week after his election, and it is recorded that he was among those who commented on the paper which compared Christianity and Islam. When asked what subject they would like to debate, the two new members announced that on Christmas Eve they would debate the proposition that the Moderates have more just views of Christianity than the Evangelicals. There was nothing quite so exhilarating as tackling problems head on.

A week later, on 17 December, Moncrieff returned to the offensive by speaking at the Theological Society on 'The insufficiency of preaching the morality of the Gospel without the doctrines', an attack on what he understood to be the chief deficiency of Moderate preaching. By this time his magazine had provoked the revival of the old student newspaper which was both smaller and cheaper than its rival. *The Argus: Seria mixta Jocis* announced in its first number that its purpose was 'opposition of a jocular kind' to the *St. Andrews Magazine*.

On 17 December, too, appeared the second number of the 'Tari' as it was by then popularly known. Its leading article was written by Henry Craik and was provocatively entitled 'Missions – Methodists – Moderates'. He had earlier asked Chalmers if he should publish it. Some, he said, 'feared its asperity', but apparently Chalmers did not veto it. Craik's argument was highly defensive: he accused his 'cold adversaries' of 'trite and meaningless raillery' and he dared them 'to the arena of argument and feeling, and we ask only that they will engage with earnestness in the conflict'.

Duff and Stewart did battle as promised on 24 December. That it was a disaster is clear from the following entry in the minutes:

Three voted for the High Flyers, one for the Moderates and thirteen declined giving their opinion on the ground either that the terms of the debate were such as did not admit of any decision, or that the subject was highly improper and ought never to have been proposed for discussion.

The constant conflict took its toll. Asperity did not come naturally to Henry Craik, and after Christmas he was plunged into despair. The spectre of atheism haunted him. On 28 December 1825 he confided in his diary:

Is the Christian religion really true? . . . What would I give to become a steady, renewed believer! Am I not the worst of hypocrites, who can mix in the society and the conversation of Christians, and who am yet utterly destitute of spiritual desire, or even of faith? . . . O God, send Thy Spirit into my heart . . . Give me more to read Thy Word.

When Craik was wallowing in despondency, John Urquhart came to his aid, reassuring him and spending time with him. Craik's admiration for Urquhart knew no bounds. He found the lad 'interesting, estimable, and engaging'. Urquhart gave him what he needed most – perfect familiarity – so that Craik could afford to relax and be himself, a lonely nineteen-year-old who found friendship difficult. Through his love for Urquhart, Craik was led through such a re-examination of his faith and hopes that he afterwards concluded that he had not before been truly converted to Christ.

On 31 December 1825 the even-handed 'Tari' published a critique of Craik's leading article. The anonymous author was a self-confessed Moderate. In fact it was Alexander Melville, who became a member of the missionary society. His article is interesting for two reasons. He does not indulge in bashing 'Methodistical enthusiasts'. Instead he is concerned to correct Evangelical misapprehensions about the Moderates – a sign that the tide was turning and that the Moderates rather than the Evangelicals would have the harder task to justify themselves. He also made the important point that an enthusiastic disposition in religious matters is frequently a matter of personality. 'That every man should be an enthusiast is impossible from the very constitution of the human mind.' It was not an entirely valid argument, since Urquhart and Moncrieff were not by nature enthusiasts, even if Duff was. But Craik was impressed by the conciliatory nature of Melville's critique.

In the fifth number of the 'Tari' published on 28 January 1826, Craik apologised for his earlier 'spirit of bitterness and sarcastic intolerance'. 'We are well aware,' he wrote, 'that no one will leave his own opinion and become a convert to ours, unless other forces are applied to him than those of ridicule and raillery.' The same number reported the outcome of a visit by a student delegation headed by Duff to the Universities Commission then visiting St. Andrews. The students had asked if it were possible to choose a Rector from outside the four professors. The Commission had replied in the negative, so the students then asked to be allowed to examine for themselves the ancient statutes of the University on which these disagreeable decisions were based. Again, Duff was one of the students chosen to conduct this investigation. The Evangelical students seemed every bit as implicated in the great rebellion as others. Duff, in particular, was always at the barricades when the cause was right. It mattered not whether the cause was 'religious' or political. The merest hint of injustice was sufficient to evoke his crusading zeal.

On 4 February 1826 a significant discussion took place in the Theological Society on 'the principal causes which have retarded the propagation of Christianity'. When the President called for a vote on the issue it was found that eleven members thought that the best way of Christianising the heathen was to send missionaries, while only three dissented. The Evangelical Party was by now not only managing to get its favourite issues debated, but it was actually winning the debates as well. A week later David Ewart was elected a member of the Theological Society without difficulty. He kept up the Evangelical presence which was weakened by the resignation of William Sinclair Mackay, another of the St. Andrews Six, who had been a member of the Society for the two sessions 1824/25 and 1825/26.

The eighth and last number of the *St. Andrews Magazine* appeared on 18 March 1826. Mitigating the embarrassment caused by its early demise was the fact that its rival, *The Argus*, had collapsed a month earlier. The 'Tari' confessed that the 'editorial pericranium' was empty as they had become over-involved in rows over the election of the Rector. The student committee, headed by their valiant champion, Duff, had investigated the musty records of the University. Duff announced the committee's findings. The students had not been misled by the professors. There was no plot. But the student lobby did manage to extend the number of eligible voters to include first- and second-year Arts students who had been disenfranchised illegally.

It only remained to witness the pomp of the election which was marred by one renegade student who persisted in asking questions in English while the professors attempted to conduct proceedings in Latin. The result was the greatest linguistic confusion since Babel. Thus the row which had stirred student disaffection for the entire session was brought to an undignified close.

The election fiasco had set student against student and heightened old tensions between Moderates and High Flyers. But there is little doubt that the chief cause of conflict was the concerted offensive mounted by the Evangelical students themselves. Duff's prominence was a problem. He had assumed the headship of the missionary society and was never to relinquish it until he left St. Andrews in 1829. Far more threatening, he was beginning to dominate the Theological Society as well. Before the Evangelical invasion members had discussed the 'science of theology' with detachment, now heat was engendered in all the debates. Even worse, Duff appeared to be at once the most scholarly as well as the most fervent of members. Just three weeks after his disastrous debate with the Moderate, Stewart, he read a learned paper on the use of the Greek article as evidence of the divinity of Christ.

The missionary society itself was the most formidable weapon in the Evangelical armoury, encouraging evangelism, recruiting members rapidly so that it was easily the largest student society, and challenging all students with the needs of the mission fields. The *St. Andrews Magazine* also served its purpose. It may have been a 'dull and lumbering miscellany', but it advertised both the town and the student missionary societies, fostered debate, gave an Evangelical perspective on literature and history, and, through a well-written serial by John Urquhart, presented a strong case for foreign missions.

Much of the persecution inflicted on the Evangelical students was a defence mechanism on the part of other students who felt they were being besieged. But, as Craik explained, there was no way that the Evangelicals could leave their uncommitted fellow-students unchallenged. If persecution resulted, that was only to be expected. The adherents of Evangelicalism have been persecuted from its birth, as have all those who 'live godly in Christ Jesus' (2 Timothy 3:12).

Perhaps greater maturity might have averted some of this persecution. But it was more important to express evangelising energy in 'great and systematic exertion' and run the risk of provoking reprisals, than to achieve nothing through an easy-going tolerance. A mature tolerance would develop inevitably with experience and the growth of spiritual discernment. Zeal might not. Far better, then, to begin a life of service to Christ as a zealot.

Nor should it be denied that the conflict between the Moderates and the High-Flyers was creative. Each was learning from the other, and the learning process was not confined to St. Andrews. Throughout Scotland relations between Moderates and Evangelicals were improving. The missionary movement, itself, encouraged each party to be more open to the other. Indeed, the Scottish missionary movement may be seen as an amalgamation of the Moderate emphasis on education and the Evangelical insistence on the proclamation of the Gospel.[1] The proposal for an educational mission to India unanimously endorsed by the General Assembly in 1824 was the brain child of the leader of the Moderate party, Dr. John Inglis. But he could at first find no-one with the required combination of talent and zeal to implement his scheme. He was not to know that, throughout his five-year-long search, suitable agents were being refined in the crucible of controversy among the students of the St. Andrews University.

[1] H. Watt, *Thomas Chalmers and the Disruption*, Edinburgh, 1943, p. 7.

'*From seven to nine in the evening I am engaged with J. Urquhart in collecting, under specific heads, all possible information on the subject of missions, both from Scriptures, under the titles of precepts – prophecies – promises – and examples, and from all other books whatever we can lay our hands on; the object of this is, with our united prayers, to seek a sober determination of the enquiry, whether or not we ought to embark in this enterprise.*'

JOHN ADAM (22 November 1825)

John Adam

8

'A Sober Determination' – The Missionary Call

Throughout the exciting session of 1825/26 Urquhart and Adam were not prominent gladiators in either the political or theological arena of conflict. Most of the Evangelical students were content to defend the faith and the missionary cause from attack. Their chief spokesman, Duff, had not yet imagined that his duty might lie beyond the frontiers of defence and controversy.

Urquhart and Adam, however, began to perceive that the Lord might be calling them to personal engagement in overseas missions. The so-called 'friends of missions' must be faced with the challenge to act for Christ as well as talk. So, with the din of the student rebellion echoing in his ears, Urquhart sat down doggedly to pen the most challenging essay ever presented to the missionary society. The process which culminated in Urquhart's great address must now be traced.

The friendship formed by Adam and Urquhart at their first meeting shortly before the foundation of the missionary society ripened quickly into a remarkably deep relationship. In the 1824/25 session they accompanied one another to Chalmers' classes, studied the Greek New Testament together, and laboured side-by-side in Sunday school work. Like others, including Chalmers, Adam was impressed first by Urquhart's academic ability, then by his mature insight, and then by his spirituality for which Adam knew no equal. In the summer of 1825 Urquhart returned to his own family in Perth and, away from his St. Andrews friends, fretted with loneliness. Adam stayed at St. Andrews for a few months in the Summer of 1825 and, to comfort Urquhart in his loneliness, wrote long letters from which the following, with its interesting reference to their mutual friend, Alexander Duff, is an extract:

[67]

St. Andrews, May 30, 1825

My very dear Friend,

Since your departure, and that of my brother and all our good friends, I have not felt so dull as might have been expected, and in truth, I have rather looked upon my solitude as a privilege. For as the time of my giving myself up to the ministerial office draws nearer and nearer, I feel more and more the importance of much heart-searching and communion with God, lest it should be found in the end I have run before I was sent, and have not received my commission directly from him. . . .

I get an hour or two every day with Mr. Duff, when we read Campbell's Lectures, the Greek Testament, and Antiquities. He and I accord very well: I should feel happy if I could be in any way useful in turning his classical enthusiasm towards the Bible and the great concerns of Religion. In the course of our reading we touch upon a great variety of subjects, as you and I did during the winter, upon which I look back with great pleasure. All this together with my out-door labours, keeps me from stagnation, and upon the whole, pretty well fills up my time. I feel quite as a bird at liberty, now that I have got free from the Mathematics, and am able to direct every thing towards the one great object. I give an hour pretty regularly to Hebrew, on which you know I lay great stress, and with which I aspire to become familiar. . . .

I think we should be very careful to improve the summer months with a particular reference to the Bible and the state of our hearts. You are not ignorant of the engrossing and absorbing effect of all human studies, and how apt they are to jostle aside into a corner the great concerns of Eternity; and I think, it is but just that now religion should have the preference. Buchanan's rule was, when he found himself more than ordinarily interested in his studies, to cast aside his books and commence praying, that thus his best hours might be given to God.

In autumn Adam returned to his large and happy family in London. October 1825 was the golden month of his friendship with Urquhart, who travelled by sea to London and stayed with Adam's family.

'The lad', then seventeen, was a great hit: Adam senior treated him as an adopted son, and one of Adam's many sisters whispered to her brother in awed tones that hitherto she had only read of people like John Urquhart. Adam was melted by Urquhart's prayers and told himself without envy that in his understanding he was a child beside Urquhart, though much his senior in years. In fact they brought out the best in each other. Urquhart's pensive spirit was cheered and animated by Adam's playfulness, and their combined talents sparked off exhilarating conversation, much to the delight of a household already famous for garrulity.

Urquhart's chief purpose in coming to London, however, was not to indulge his friendship with Adam. Feeling that the Lord might be calling him to serve overseas, Urquhart wished to investigate openings with the London Missionary Society and, in particular, to visit Dr. Morrison, then home for a year from his labours in China. It was in itself an important part of the lad's education to meet the great missionary and discover that he was neither charming nor enthusiastic. On the contrary Morrison was blunt to the point of rudeness, a characteristic which Urquhart rightly attributed to his disdain of the niceties of an age grown effeminate through over-refinement. Urquhart was also impressed that Morrison did not insist on the over-riding importance of his own sphere of responsibility. Nevertheless, he lent Urquhart a Chinese dictionary valued at the enormous sum of 13 guineas, presented him with a copy of his *Chinese Miscellany*, and set him to the study of Chinese.

Thus equipped, Urquhart and Adam sailed north to commence the 1825/26 session, their last session at St. Andrews. They resolved to study Chinese together and to examine the Scriptures more closely and prayerfully than ever, so that they might come to a final conclusion about their future. By now the chief question for both of them was whether they would become missionaries or, instead, enter a theological college to train for the ministry.

So, while most of their fellow-students plotted rebellion in bunks or public houses (aided by liquor), or tied themselves in meta-physical knots in the Theological Society, Adam and Urquhart were engaged in a more sober enterprise.

Robert Nesbit, too, was oblivious to all the excitement at St. Andrews for he was by now tutor to a private family far away in Exeter in the south of England. As Adam and Urquhart together willingly explored God's purpose for their lives, Nesbit wrestled unwillingly and alone against a persistent call to the mission field. The result was that half the St. Andrews Six resolved to accept the call to missionary service at about the same time.

For Urquhart and Adam the determination to become mission-aries was a decisive affirmation of a deeply-felt need, but it was also the culmination of impressive research. Each evening between the hours of seven and nine they conducted their systematic enquiry. Adam wrote:

We applied ourselves . . . to a thorough investigation of every thing relating to missions. For this purpose we searched the sacred Scriptures, and summed up our inquiries under the heads of *precepts, prophecies, examples,* and *promises.* We also perused Brown's History of Missions; Horne's, Ward's, Milne's, and Judson's Letters; the Lives of Martyn (. . . read repeatedly . . .), Brainerd and Chamberlain; Ward's History of the Hindoos, etc.

Urquhart described his decision in a long letter to William Orme who was now pastor of a London Church and foreign secretary of the London Missionary Society:

Mr. Adam and [I] have made the subject of missions a matter of daily consideration this session; and after deliberately viewing all sides of the question, and candidly comparing the claims of our home population and the Heathen world, and earnestly seeking for direction from Him who has promised to be the guide of His people, even unto death, I have come to the final resolution of devoting myself to the service of God among the Heathen. I have made the history of missions, and the biography of missionaries, a part of my daily study, for some time, and have perused, I think, nearly all the principal works on the subject. And I am glad I have done so; for it has given me much sounder views of the matter than I had before.

Urquhart's letter is dated 10 March 1826. On the same day Adam gave an address to the missionary society entitled 'On personally Engaging in the Work of Missions'. In it he announced his own decision to become a missionary and concluded, 'If it be but for the name of Jesus, all shall be well, and I am persuaded that on a death bed, it will not cost us one regret, to have forsaken all for Christ.'

Eighty students gathered on 3 April 1826 to hear Urquhart deliver his presidential address. The passions of the rectorship controversy had subsided, and the students little suspected that there was another drop of excitement to be wrung from the 1825/26 session. Perhaps they had grown accustomed to the missionary society meeting as a retreat from confrontation, for there no criticism or debate was permitted. They were soon painfully aware that there was a much wider divide between themselves and their earnest speaker than that which separated them from their confessed opponents.

Urquhart was the friend of all present. Not one had ever thought ill of him. Many had been profoundly helped by him in times of spiritual crisis. He knew that he could say what he liked to them, and he used this great advantage to bring home to his fellow Christians that they were in danger, like all the half-hearted, of forfeiting the friendship of Christ (Revelation 3·16).

As Duff later recalled, Urquhart's abrupt introduction instantaneously aroused general attention: 'I am tired of arguing with the opponents of the missionary cause. It is my intention this evening to address myself to those who profess to be its friends.'

Urquhart perceived that, in the self-congratulatory atmosphere of many a missionary meeting, it was difficult to resist the temptation to smugness when labelled 'a friend to missions'. He refused to flatter his hearers. Instead he advanced the 'unpalatable doctrine' that 'the members of missionary associations have absolutely done nothing, when we consider the high demands of a cause whose object is the spiritual and moral renovation of a world'.

Urquhart also sought to avoid the 'colouring of romance' so common at missionary meetings. Romantic idealism appealed to the imagination but 'failed to influence the conduct'. In fact it had provided the 'friends of missions' with an excuse for not engaging personally in the work. They had argued that this work was too high for them; that it was for those super-sacrificing types with a strong faith. But, countered Urquhart, 'the test of simple discipleship', not super-discipleship, is found in the words of Christ, 'If any man come to me and hate not his father and mother, and wife and children, and brethren and sisters, yea, and his own life also, he cannot be my disciple.' He who shrinks from duty, when contemplating the trials of a missionary life, is not suffering from weak faith, but from the absence of faith. It is not that he is a weak disciple; rather he is not a disciple at all.

During the course of his researches with Adam, Urquhart had become convinced of the need to remove the aura of romanticism surrounding the missionary movement. At first he had been disappointed to discover that missionaries were men of like infirmities with other Christians. Adam helped him to see, however, that weakness was no bar to Christian service, since 'all instruments are alike in an Almighty hand'.

Because, in the course of his research, Urquhart had discovered so many instances of apostasy among missionaries he had come almost to welcome opposition. 'For surely if our desire for the work cannot stand against the remonstrances of our friends, we have every reason to think it would soon be quenched amid the heavy and lengthened discouragements which must be met with in the work itself.'

Malan had alerted Adam to the possibility that in the young a desire for missionary service could originate in *un trait de l'imagination*, and Urquhart conceded that there was 'much of romance' in his first desire to become a missionary. 'But,' he had written in March 1826, 'I trust the detail of facts which have come under my review, has done much to dissipate this; and has, at the same time impressed me more deeply than ever with the duty of engaging in this department of the ministerial work.' Through his research, then, romanticism had evaporated and his sense of duty had strengthened. It is therefore not surprising that as Urquhart began his address by disowning romanticism, he also stressed the primacy of duty as a motive to missionary service – the duty of obeying the great commission (Matthew 28:18–20).

Not content with the insinuation that many friends of missions were really not disciples at all, Urquhart demonstrated the heinousness of the attitude that it is better to do a little for the cause of missions than nothing at all. For to do a little is to recognise the reality of the need in such a way as to ease one's own conscience rather than the sufferings of the needy.

It is not enough to give money, he urged. The coffers of the missionary societies have never been so full, because it had become fashionable to support missions. Yet, he reasoned, missionary zeal was probably actually declining since all the great societies – the Scottish Missionary Society, the London and Church Missionary Societies, even the Moravians – were finding it more difficult than ever to recruit missionaries.

Here Urquhart was in agreement with the Moderate critique of Craik's article on 'Missions – Methodists – Moderates' in the *St. Andrews Magazine*. Melville had written, 'From its having of late become a fashionable thing to attend Missionary Societies, and teach Sabbath Schools I am afraid that there is nowadays much more religion in the mouths, than in the hearts of those who call themselves Christians.' Urquhart was afraid of that, too, and he observed that as soon as the duty of personal engagement in missions is mentioned, even the most ardent supporters suddenly discover a host of objections which they would otherwise be quick to refute. The chief cause of their reluctance was the love which bound them to their families. Urquhart conceded that this love was 'perhaps the strongest passion . . . in the human breast'. 'And ' he added, 'Christianity, far from impairing, refines and strengthens the attachment':

There is but one, and only one *Being*, in the universe, whom we are to love with a stronger affection. It is little wonder then, that where feelings like these – so strong, that no time or distance can ever efface their influence; and so pure, that piety itself imparts to them a tone of deeper tenderness – exert an opposing influence, even most decided Christians should be startled at the first proposal of a duty which speaks destruction to them all.

Behind Urquhart's sensitivity to this issue which was a great problem for so many missionaries, was the pain of his own family situation. Urquhart's parents were far from intolerant of his religious inclinations, but they felt deeply the prospect of parting with their son probably for ever as the missionary mortality rate was then very high. Nothing in the prospect of separation caused Urquhart greater distress than the prospect of causing further grief to his parents, who had so recently lost another son. He was, therefore, very grateful to his mother, and apparently not a little surprised, when she spoke to him on the subject with calm and resignation. 'I could wish much to soothe the declining years of that dear friend, who watched over my helpless infancy,' he had written to her tenderly. 'I would like to be able to make some return for the anxious hours, and the sleepless nights, I have cost you. This I may never have in my power; but wherever my lot be cast, I shall never forget the tenderness of a mother's love.'

This he had written on 14 February 1826 shortly after reaching his final decision to become a missionary. In the same packet of letters he had enclosed one to his last remaining brother, David, a letter preceded and followed with prayer and written in tears. Urquhart had no certainty that his brother was a Christian, and, after entreating him to accept the Gospel, had written:

I confess that, in the prospect of leaving my parents, one half of the great burden that lies upon my mind would be removed, could I confidently rely on the religious principles of my sister, and especially of yourself, who, in a short time, will be their *only son*, and almost their only earthly protector.

He could have avoided all this pain by staying. Why then did he still feel constrained to go? Here Urquhart came to the heart of his address. 'The main argument on which I would insist is founded on the commandment of our Saviour; Go ye and teach all nations.' Urquhart knew that this command – 'the great commission' – had been reiterated so often by missionary advocates that it had 'lost something of its freshness' even if it had 'lost nothing of its force'. Yet he had a totally fresh application to make: 'Not only do I look upon this little verse as the great foundation on which all arguments for missions must be received, but as the only scriptural authority which we can have for preaching the gospel at all.' Men were attracted to the ministry in Britain by many inducements, but their only valid authority was this commission. It is only as Great Britain is one of the 'all nations' specified in this commission that anyone is authorised to preach the Gospel there:

Grant me but this view of the subject, and the question comes home with irresistible force. How comes it that all the labourers should have continued to cluster together in one little corner of the vineyard? ... in what does the vast superiority of its claims consist?

There was nothing in the great commission which justified such an unequal distribution of labourers. The attractions of holding ministerial office in Britain – civilised comforts and refinements, opportunities for literary or scientific work, the security of a benefice in the Established churches, or the excitement of helping the progress of nonconformist denominations – had little to do with the Great Commission. Strip Britain of these extraneous attractions, Urquhart challenged his hearers, and then tell me what justification there is for its monopoly of Gospel ministers.

Urquhart's understanding of the universality of the Gospel had undermined the parochialism which fettered the imagination of his fellows. To counter further their prejudice, he asked them to imagine the following situation. God commanded that, instead of the world, a single country, Great Britain, should be the object of the great commission. All the Christians, however, chose to dwell in just one Scottish county, Mid Lothian, and made no effort to evangelise the remainder of Britain, except by collecting money, and sending two or three preachers to itinerate throughout the length and breadth of the land. Then even these few evangelists were exhausted and the need arose to replace them. Some suitable evangelists said this was not the proper time to be evangelising even though the Lord had promised to be with his missionaries always in the work to which they were commissioned. Others said that the earlier evangelists had not pursued a wise plan, as if the error of some is an excuse for the disobedience of others.

Still others argued that to kindle the flame of missionary enthusiasm for the rest of Britain would dampen the fires in Mid Lothian. This argument, too, conflicted with known facts: those most zealous for the propagation of the Gospel abroad were most zealous for its propagation at home; school, tract, itinerant, and home mission societies had all been established by the supporters of foreign missions.

Finally there were those who said that they could not venture further afield while there were still some in Mid Lothian who were unconverted. They said this in spite of professing belief in the doctrine of election which states that the redeemed would be gathered 'out of every kindred and tongue, and people, and nation', thus demonstrating that it is false to expect that all in a particular nation will ever be converted. Urquhart thus demonstrated that the doctrine of election, far from being a barrier to missionary zeal as some opponents of Calvinism. asserted, was a great incentive to world-wide evangelism. This point is so important that it is worth quoting at length from a letter which Adam wrote to Urquhart the previous Summer showing how the two friends had forged together these elements in their case for foreign missions:

> St. Andrews, 18 July 1825
> I quite accord with you upon the subject of missions, and think that the fact of leaving unconverted persons at home . . . is no objection to our carrying the Gospel to Heathen lands. I was particularly struck with the view you took of God's *gathering* his people, not exclusively from this or that particular country, but from all the families of the earth. So it is said in Revelation, 'every kindred and tongue,' &c. The declaration of our Lord to his Apostles was, that they should be brought before kings for a *witness*, which I think perfectly accords with your view, that the Gospel is to be preached to all nations, that 'one of a city, and two of a family' (tribe I suppose) are to be selected as He may see best, as monuments of his sparing mercy: and then we have no warrant for supposing that whole nations, cities, villages, or even families, are in any period likely to be all converted. It is contrary to God's own declarations, to the analogy of his past and present dispensations, to what we have read in history, and what we see daily before our eyes. That command also of our Saviour, 'if they receive you not in one city, flee ye to another,' intimates the same thing. So that whilst there is one city which has not had 'the good news of the kingdom' proclaimed in its streets, so long do I think missionary exertions are our

bounden duty – and so long will it become those who are putting their hand to the Gospel plough, to enquire conscientiously before God, whether it be more for his glory, and more consonant with his will, that their labours should be directed towards that as yet uncultivated desert, or merely to spend their days in watering and training the gardens which have long been tended by the care of many skilful and efficient labourers. The example of the Apostles is also quite conclusive.

So treated, Urquhart's Mid Lothian illustration expanded into a forceful parable which demonstrated how illogical was the opposition to personal involvement in overseas missions. It showed how feeble the church had been in fulfilment of its mandate: in the Gospel the church had the means to renovate the world, but did not seem to be even interested in the world. It exposed that emotion, misnamed patriotism, which consisted not so much in love of one's own country as in despising and ignoring every other. It brought home to his hearers that the world was the mission field and that Christians were unwarranted in circumscribing the great commission:

The whole human race forms but one little family in the universe of God . . . Are we not united by the ties of a common nature? Are we not involved in a common calamity, in that we have forfeited the favour of our God . . .? And is not a common pardon offered, and has not a common Saviour died for us all?

Urquhart concluded his robust manifesto of the universality of the Christian faith with the announcement of his own resolution:

As I have proceeded with my inquiries on the subject, the difficulties seemed to have gathered thicker on the prospect, but the convictions of duty have grown stronger, too. The arguments for personal engagement seem to me to have acquired the strength of a demonstration. I have therefore, resolved, with the help of God, to devote my life to the cause; and I have only solemnly to charge every one of you, who are looking forward to the ministry of Christ, to take this matter into most serious consideration.

It is difficult to credit accounts of the impact of this address. The recent testimony of the Scandinavian scholar, O. G. Mykelbust, who has made an exhaustive study of missionary education, might disarm the over-incredulous. He has described Urquhart's address as 'an eloquent appeal, one of the ablest on record, to . . . students on the subject of foreign missions'. Myklebust's assessment is based purely on a reading of the words and an analysis of the argument. How much greater must the impact have been on those who, like Duff, witnessed Urquhart's eyes aglow 'with wistful longing and fervent entreaty' and who heard his mellow voice trembling with emotion. The response was more than admiration. Here were 'thoughts that breathe, and words that burn'.

Even Craik was lost for words as that night he wrote in his diary, 'I do not know how to speak of this Essay. It displayed greater power than ever even Mr. Urquhart had exhibited before. . . . My feelings after its delivery were too strong for utterance.' With the return of his powers of articulation, Craik wrote up the minutes of the meeting:

Never probably in any association has such an address on such a subject been before delivered. To say that it was most eloquent – most solemn – most affecting – the production of a mind of mighty grasp sedulously and continuously directed to one single object of mightiest import may convey to those who heard it not some idea of the impression produced by it.

Craik's effusions, however, were nothing compared with the sincere rhapsody written forty years later by the witness perhaps most influenced by Urquhart's address, Alexander Duff:

The combined effect of the whole might well be said to have been over-whelming. For a moment it appeared as if all present were ready to rise up and march forth as a united phalanx into the battle field; and few there were who did not then at least resolve to submit the subject to an examin-ation with which it had never been honoured before; while of some, it can be added that they did not pause till they found themselves across oceans and continents, in front of the bristling hosts and frowning citadels of heathenism.

However emotional, then, the initial reaction to Urquhart's great address, there is no doubting that its impact was permanent. With remorseless logic and brilliant, memorable analogies, Urquhart had touched the nerve of commitment in all his hearers. Only one thing seemed to matter: to discover God's will and do it.

'*We may be gaining new victories over* the devil, the world and the flesh, *even while here. Let it be our earnest endeavour to maintain this holy warfare within our breasts; and while we drink freely of the fountain of life, let us not forget to present its waters to that world which is* "dead *in trespasses and sins*".'

JOHN URQUHART (30 June 1826)

9

Charity Begins at Home

The spiritual movement at St. Andrews, culminating in Urquhart's memorable address, created a great need among the Evangelical students to discover what God wanted them to do with their lives. Their growing commitment to overseas missions was accompanied by an intensification of interest in evangelistic work in their own university and town.

This greater courage for the work of God at home and abroad was accompanied by a desire for greater insight into the mind of God, since a willingness to do something for God is no guarantee that God wants it done. The St. Andrews students, however, were in no doubt that one way to discover the will of God is to experiment.

Chalmers' St. Andrews was a veritable laboratory for evangelistic experiments. The Doctor held a Sunday-school class in his own house and through it reached out to parents. In the session of conflict, 1825/26, he entrusted the class to Urquhart, and not only reviewed his teaching over supper each Sunday evening, but also trained Urquhart in the skills of visitation, as together they called on parents, the poor, and the sick. 'This is what I call preaching the Gospel to every creature,' he explained to Urquhart as they walked from house to house. 'That cannot be done by setting yourself up in a pulpit, as a centre of attraction, but by going forth and making aggressive movements upon the community, and by preaching from house to house.'

While admitting that a visit to every family by a 'Christian philanthropist' was the ideal, Urquhart was developing a taste for the practical, and he observed that Chalmers' scheme was inadequate. There were not enough labourers. So in this same session 'a new system' was tried. The favourably disposed in every corner of the town were asked to allow their neighbours to meet in their homes to hear the Gospel. Sometimes fifty or sixty people attended, many of whom never entered a church. Chalmers had to admit that while not up to his ideal, this scheme was far more effective than 'common preaching', adding in a typical simile: 'It was like carrying about the magnet, and bringing it near to the iron filings.'

Some of the experiments owed more to the unbounded enthusiasm unleashed by Chalmers than to common sense. Henry Craik, raised to dizzy heights of idealism by Chalmers' lectures in the 1824/25 session, proposed an ambitious scheme to the Doctor. He, Duff, and two others would stay in St. Andrews over the summer months of 1825 and commence a school, offering 'gratuitous instruction' in moral and political science, mathematics and natural philosophy to the 'lower orders'. In a sense this putative university for the hoi-polloi did materialise – not in St. Andrews in 1825, but in Calcutta in 1830.

Chalmers' St. Andrews was one of dreams and visions and schemes, but it was not one of fantasy. The present must not be overlooked in laying schemes for the future, insisted Urquhart. Souls are perishing now. They will not start to perish when, at some distant time, we are fully equipped to meet their needs. Such urgency is implicit in the Gospel and it was reinforced in Urquhart's mind by the example of his closest friend.

When John Adam had arrived in St. Andrews in November 1824 he surveyed the scene. The near-by villages, he concluded, were in need of Gospel preaching, and sailors and fishermen, in particular, were deprived of opportunities to hear the Gospel by the exigencies of their work. By the end of the 1824/25 session Adam had established three village centres to expound the Scriptures on Sundays, and a fourth on Wednesdays in St. Andrews for the fishermen. To one of these, Dunino, where four millennia earlier Celtic hunters celebrated their pagan rituals, Adam invited Urquhart to assist him. Conscious of his youth Urquhart would only pray and read, leaving the preaching to Adam.

This work was Adam's chief delight. His hearers followed his expositions carefully in their own Bibles. Adam recalled that Whitefield when preaching in Scotland had been impressed when so many turned pages of the Scriptures that it was like the rustling of leaves in the wind. Adam was also thrilled to preach in Crail, ten miles from St. Andrews, for here, almost three centuries earlier, John Knox had stirred the people with his preaching.

These labours were sustained in the 1825/26 session. Adam usually preached twice every Sunday and walked about ten miles which, he said, was excellent for his health. Neither rain nor snow would stop him. To his friends who spoke of the dangers of such exposure, he replied that he was anxious to acquire 'a hardihood of constitution' so that he could withstand 'the still greater privations and hardships of a Missionary life'.

At the end of the 1825/26 session, following their decision to become missionaries, Adam and Urquhart proposed their most ambitious scheme to date: a tour of the English-speaking parts of the Highlands on an evangelistic mission. 'We wish,' explained Adam, 'to make a little experiment before entering on large fields of labour.'

The wish was not granted. Urquhart fell ill. Throughout the summer of 1826 his sickness lingered and was accompanied by severe depression. A warning of his condition had been sounded in the 1825/26 session when he suffered a fit of depression far more severe than the remorse common to devout and scrupulous souls. Then he had doubted if he really was a child of God. He feared he was going insane. It had all been rather inexplicable and frightening.

Under this pressure an interesting feature of his personality emerged. Hitherto he appeared always cheerful and serene, if earnest and determined. Many friends, most of them older than he, sought and followed his advice. Yet he was far more dependent on them than they were on him. Without close and deep Christian friendship he was so lonely he could hardly bear it. John Adam realised this and advised him to avoid too much solitude.

Solitude, however, was the chief feature of Urquhart's experience in the summer and autumn of 1826. In May he consented to his father's wish to take up a tutor's position in the house of Colonel Morland near Glasgow. He proved a conscientious tutor for Morland's ten-year-old son, inspired rather than burdened by the thought that he was moulding a mind which would bear the imprint of his influence for all eternity. Urquhart also had plenty of spare time for his own studies and spent it mainly on the Scriptures in Hebrew and Greek. But he was lonely.

On 7 July 1826, his eighteenth birthday, he was fatigued to the point of exhaustion and wrote nothing in his diary. The next day he managed to record his gratitude to God for eighteen years of blessings, but he was troubled with severe headache. A month later he was still missing the 'little circle' at St. Andrews, but, he wrote, 'these are sinful thoughts'. Far better to follow Whitefield's brave advice and attempt to make Christians where he could not find any. So he visited the few cottages around Colonel Morland's house, established a young men's society, and treated its fourteen members to fervent evangelistic essays.

Still he fretted for his St. Andrews friends. His emotional dependence on them troubled him. A Christian, he thought, has access to the throne of grace and should be immune from external circumstances. How sinful, then, he reasoned, to be despondent! That must be it – sin! 'Sin will damp the most glorious hopes, and unbelief will render unavailing the most precious promises.' At other moments, the suffering Urquhart glimpsed a different truth. Despondency might be a cause of spiritual weakness rather than its fruit. 'Mental depression,' he wrote 'is ten-fold more distressing than bodily disease. The latter often adds to spiritual comfort; the former generally destroys it.'

Urquhart's burden was not eased by Craik who throughout the summer of 1826 was plunged again into a long dark night of doubt. He feared that, against his will, his religious pilgrimage would terminate in atheism since he found unbearable the consideration that in the Christian scheme millions of people seemed to be created for 'a moment's giddy pleasure, and then an eternity of unmingled wretchedness'. In his weakened condition, Urquhart was susceptible to Craik's gloom, but he mustered sufficient strength to appeal to his friend:

O do not talk of the *unwilling* rejection of a God! All Atheists are wilful Atheists. This I must believe, while I believe the Bible. God has had some end in view, my dear friend, in giving you up to these dreadful thoughts.

Urquhart began to discover a purpose behind his own dreadful thoughts. He was learning more of 'the preciousness and sufficiency of the Saviour' and he was, he thought for the first time, becoming acquainted with himself. And what was he? He was, he perceived, an exotic hot-house Christian who wilted alarmingly when exposed to a hostile climate. 'In some respects,' he observed, 'the very fact of having enjoyed a religious education, makes that time more critically dangerous, when you begin to enjoy it no longer.'

The lowest point of Urquhart's mental sufferings was reached on the morning of 18 July 1826. His depression was so vicious that he feared he was in the grip of Satan himself. Near panic, he struggled to pray and then took a ride in a carriage, hoping the fresh breeze would clear his mind of torment. But, he wrote, 'the malady raged with greater violence, so as almost to make me dread real madness'. Then the attack passed, and he was left in tranquillity, recalling the earlier part of the day as if it had all been a nightmare.

Shaken by the ferocity of the assault, he searched for an explanation. Perhaps the Lord had given him over like Job and Peter to be tested by Satan. Had Jesus prayed for him, Urquhart wondered, as He had for Peter that his faith would not fail? Perhaps, he thought, returning to the problem which would not go away, his dependence on his friends was excessive.

It is well, when we hasten after other lovers, that He, who will have our whole heart, should hedge up our way. And when he leads us into the *wilderness*, and dries up many a source of what seemed *holy* enjoyment, it is often not to punish, but to help us, to 'speak comfortably' to us.

Nevertheless, he was carried through the remainder of July by the thought that he was just about to 'unbosom freely' all his feelings to his 'dear John Adam'. He was almost amused to observe himself postponing writing for the most trifling reasons. Clearly the major reason was 'the desire to indulge this pleasing expectation a little longer'. On 2 August 1826 he thus described his chief anxiety to Adam:

You know me too well to require me to tell you how I feel, without a single Christian friend near. The harp has been often out of tune; and sometimes, I have feared that its strings were about to break, when the Lord has again tuned it to his own praise . . . I thought I could leave all, and live happy in a solitary desert, for the sake of Christ. But I find that much of my happiness was drawn from cisterns, and not from the life-giving fountain. And now that the Lord has, in mercy broken these, to lead me to himself, I have been ready to weep as if my all were lost. I fear I have mistaken love to Christians for love to Christ.

Urquhart concluded this letter with a reference to the opposition of his friends to the ideas he presented in his presidential address to the missionary association at St. Andrews. But he did not wish to be misunderstood; his every prayer made him more determined than ever to become a missionary.

Adam's cheerful reply from London was dated 22 August 1826. He counselled his friend to go more frequently to Glasgow for Christian fellowship, particularly to the Congregationalist churches of Ralph Wardlaw and Greville Ewing, and not to hesitate to associate with the local, uneducated faithful, as 'it is simple Christianity you chiefly want'. He told Urquhart not to be surprised by the opposition to his missionary views: the fires of persecution had long been extinguished in Britain, and British Christians had very little understanding of what was meant by the host of biblical references which speak of suffering for Christ, of leaving all, and following him. Then he informed Urquhart that the London Missionary Society was hoping to send a well-educated missionary to a responsible position in Madras, India. Hitherto Urquhart had thought only of going to China, but Adam wrote:

What say you to a partnership? And, as two are better than one, let us offer ourselves as having one heart and one soul, to depart in two years' time, that we may live and die together. I have been furnished with many details and much information, which shall be common property as soon as the treaty is signed between us.

Urquhart tried to respond calmly to this proposal, but he was clearly elated. He lost no time in seeking his parents' approval. He was shocked, however, to discover that their earlier reluctant acceptance had changed into decided opposition. They had thought a period away from his friends would cool his ardour and were frankly disappointed to discover that his determination was firmer than ever.

They argued that his health was too feeble and that he was always catching colds. They even reminded him needlessly that his chronic headaches were a symptom of his late brother's terminal illness. The prospect of his missionary ambitions collapsing before him, the distressed Urquhart hurried back to Glasgow to seek the opinion of Dr. Cokely, physician to Colonel Morland's regiment. The doctor thought Urquhart's slight constitution more suited to the Madras climate than a stout one. This was not necessarily an encouraging opinion, but Urquhart argued that fears for his health were unjustified. His harassed parents therefore insisted that he could not go because of family circumstances.

Poor Urquhart was nonplussed. The conviction that he should

become a missionary was now so strong that he believed it was the will of God. On the Day of Judgment would the Lord excuse the contravention of His will on the grounds of youth? Urquhart was by now thoroughly weary of using youth as an excuse for putting off hard decisions. Furthermore, he had observed that the only times he felt that it might not be his duty to become a missionary were when 'the chilling influence of the world' had 'cooled every holy affection'.

He wrote to Adam on 17 September 1826 explaining that he could not quite seal the contract, secretly hoping that his friend would exhort him to follow the more courageous, if defiant, path. In fact, Urquhart, never provoked when his own interests were threatened, was capable of fierceness in the cause of the Gospel. When told that missionaries were prohibited by law from preaching in China, he had said that it would be his duty to disobey. If the consequence were death, so be it: the missionary's cause is frequently advanced more by his blood than by many years' labour. Urquhart was therefore deflated to receive Adam's reply of 7 October 1826 saying that there was really only one thing he could do – wait. Adam confessed that he had always found the missionary's 'non-payment of the debt of gratitude' to parents 'one of the darkest aspects of the missionary question', adding that his own parents were reluctant to give their consent. He advised his friend to wait until he was 21. By then he might have persuaded another to go which would be 'more than labouring many years in the vineyard'.

Urquhart acquiesced. All was darkness and perplexity, but he recalled the words of Isaiah (42:16), 'The Lord leadeth the blind by a way that they knew not' and he was able to believe that with such a Leader, it is a privilege even to be blind. Meanwhile, he was cheered by news of Nesbit. The Scottish Missionary Society had accepted his application for service in India, he was shortly to be ordained at St. Andrews, and would have the opportunity again to challenge members of the student missionary society. Urquhart's old pastor and friend, William Orme, was also encouraging. He had written to Urquhart's father urging him to resist no longer 'a desire which seemed so evidently of God', and was convinced that when the painful time came, perhaps in a few years, for John to separate from his parents, he would no longer meet with their opposition.

On 16 November 1826 Urquhart wrote to Adam, closing the matter for the time being:

If you must go without me, I think I can bear it. All my experience tells me that I want a tried friend to lean upon . . . and such I hoped you might be to me.

Adam knew that. That is why he had suggested earlier that they should labour together in Madras, but he was not displeased when Urquhart added, 'But I see my error – I must lean upon Christ.' Adam was also glad to read:

I know nothing of that strange dejection which pressed so heavy on me before. I wish you would destroy anything I wrote to you then . . . I must have appeared to you little other than a fool or a madman . . . I do in earnest thank the Lord that I now enjoy not only health of body, but that little valued, but highly precious blessing, soundness of mind.

Urquhart enjoyed this precious blessing for three more weeks.

'May the Lord give us understanding in all things, make apparent . . . his will, guide us into the right path, strengthen our faith, consummate our holiness, and make us meet for heaven!'

JOHN ADAM (1825)

10

Consummation of Holiness

Early in December 1826 Urquhart suffered a relapse. For a week he could scarcely concentrate on his studies, any physical exertion left him breathless, and the very thought of food was nauseating. On 14 December, Colonel Morland, Urquhart's employer, asked Dr. Cokely to see Urquhart again. The doctor diagnosed a liver complaint and prescribed drastic treatment: a blister to be applied to his right side where he had suffered chronic pain, a strict diet, and a course of medicine – Down's powders and 'the blue pill', which Urquhart mistook for mercury.

Urquhart was alarmed by this fresh threat to his heart's desire and wrote in his diary:

This has distressed me a good deal, as it may unfit me for the East, which I have long contemplated as the scene of my labours. But the Lord knows what is best. If he hedge up the way, I may not walk in it. I *would* not, if I might. I begin a course of medicine on Friday, which, I pray God may bless for the restoration of my health; that my body may be fitted for his service. If this be not his will, I know that the destruction of this body will perfect the soul, and fit it for a higher, and a holier service, in the heavenly temple.

With such thoughts in mind, Urquhart replied to a letter from Craik who had written lamenting his worldliness and longing for a closer walk with God. If only he could cross the Rubicon of his present fears and doubts, Craik had supposed, how happy he would be in Jesus! Urquhart wrote, 'I remember feeling as I think you do. I thought, did I decidedly give up the hope of worldly honours and comforts, by deciding on the missionary life, I should no more be harassed by the cares, or allured by vanities of earth.' There was a temptation for all the St. Andrews Six to think like that, and indeed Robert Nesbit was to express strikingly similar views just a week later in a moving account of his missionary call to the student society at St. Andrews. But Urquhart now doubted this. 'The river of death is the Rubicon,' he wrote to Craik. 'Not till we have passed *it*, shall we be completely freed from the world, and from its cares.'

In Chalmers' lectures he had learned of the breadth of God's love, embracing all the concerns of men. In his hours of research with Adam, he explored the length of the love of God, embracing those afar off, in China and India. Now in the school of suffering he was to discover the height and depth of the love of God, and the discovery took him by surprise. He had always imagined that his prayer for spirituality of mind would be answered with light, faith, and joy. He had always thought his carefully laid plans to extend God's kingdom abroad must be realised. Now his health and his plans lay in ruins. John Newton's hymn, long precious to him, now became priceless:

> I asked the Lord that I might grow
> In faith, and love, and ev'ry grace;
> Might more of his salvation know,
> And seek more earnestly his face.
>
> I hop'd that in some favour'd hour,
> At once he'd answer my request;
> And by his love's constraining pow'r
> Subdue my sins and give me rest.
>
> Instead of this, he made me feel
> The hidden evils of my heart;
> And let the angry pow'rs of hell
> Assault my soul in ev'ry part.
>
> 'Lord, why is this?' I trembling cried;
> 'Wilt thou pursue thy worm to death?'
> ''Tis in this way', the Lord replied,
> 'I answer pray'r for grace and faith.'
>
> 'These inward trials I employ,
> From self and pride to set thee free;
> And break thy schemes of earthly joy,
> That thou may'st seek thy all in me.'

Urquhart did not post his solemn letter to Craik until Christmas Day, by which time he was able to report that the doctor now thought him free of the disease, although he was so weakened by the treatment that he could scarcely write more. On 30 December Craik wrote in his diary:

Received a letter from my dear brother Urquhart. Our Father has seen meet to afflict him with some bodily disease. Oh may He heal him, and that speedily, and make me worthy of such a friend!

But on Tuesday, 2 January 1827, Urquhart's condition worsened. He decided to leave Colonel Morland's house and return to his parents' house in Perth, although he was reluctant to reveal to them that he was very seriously ill. The next day he reached Glasgow and was so sick that the Congregationalist pastor, Greville Ewing, persuaded him to stay with him for a couple of days. On Friday, 5 January, no ticket on the coach to Perth could be procured. This agitated Urquhart, but Ewing assured him that 'there is a providence in all these things' and wrote, against Urquhart's wishes, to his father inviting him to Glasgow immediately. At 2 p.m. the next day the doctor called and asked Mrs. Ewing how he was. 'He's getting a little food down,' she replied, 'but he stares at us and does not speak.' On hearing this the doctor rushed upstairs, an alarmed Mrs. Ewing in pursuit. He looked in Urquhart's eyes, tried to get him to speak, and called for more medical assistance, diagnosing 'a very bad case of suppression on the brain'. Urquhart's head was shaved and leeches applied, followed by blisters over his head and neck.

The next morning, Sunday, Urquhart's father arrived, but John was still insensible to his surroundings and did not recognise him. Ewing returned after the morning service and prayed over the patient, after which Urquhart reached out his hand, pressed Ewing's, and smiled. 'Do you know me?' Ewing asked. Urquhart replied, 'Do not I know Mr. Ewing?' He then recognised his father and Mrs. Ewing and said, 'My mind is quite calm now . . . my hope is fixed on the Rock of Ages. I know that nothing shall separate me from the love of God, which is in Christ Jesus my Lord.'

These words, uttered with a good deal of emphasis, reduced to tears all present, including a student friend – probably William Tait. For him the joyful calm he now witnessed was an extraordinary transition in one who, he knew, had suffered severe depression so recently. Urquhart's face, he thought, was irradiated exactly as it had been when he had delivered his unforgettable address to the missionary society at St. Andrews eight months earlier. The student could not accept that Urquhart was dying, but he perceived that he was already transported above the earthly realm. He was reminded of St. Paul's words in 2 Timothy 4:6, and, that evening, under the influence of powerful emotion, wrote this poem:

> The Christian Pilgrim bid depart,
>   Departs without a sigh,
> Fear can no longer chill his heart,
>   Or sorrow dim his eye.
>
> In Heaven's own garments see him stand
>   On death's much dreaded shore,
> He gazes on the promised land,
>   And seems already o'er.
>
> We saw him oft betray a fear
>   As near this flood he drew;
> But now a willing pilgrim here,
>   He kindles at the view.
>
> A ray hath broke from Canaan's land,
>   Across that sullen flood:
> It bids him quit its mortal strand,
>   And onward march to God.
>
> He marches on, for now his eye
>   Hath lost life's lurid ray,
> As suns which quit a clouded sky
>   To shine in brighter day.
>
> Oh could we catch one moment's view,
>   Of what he now must know,
> Sorrow would fill our spirits too,
>   To linger thus below.

On Monday morning, 8 January 1827, Urquhart asked to see his father. When he came, he said, 'John, do you know your father?', and when Urquhart answered, 'Yes,' his father said, 'I hope you know your Father in heaven, who, I trust, has prepared a mansion for you.' The poor man had struggled against the prospect of losing his son to India; he hoped now that he would not have to give him up thus soon to God. But on Tuesday Urquhart's condition rapidly deteriorated and that evening, despairing of his son's recovery, the father surrendered him to God in a harrowing scene in which the father's natural yearnings wrestled with the Christian's resignation.

On Wednesday, 10 January 1827, Greville Ewing wrote to Thomas Chalmers:

Our amiable young Christian friend, Mr. John Urquhart, of whose character you spoke in so gratifying a manner, when Mrs. Ewing and I had last the pleasure of seeing you, has this day been received, we trust, into the joy of our Lord. He died, in our house, this morning at half past ten o'clock. . . . I trust it will be deeply felt among his fellow students, with whom I suppose he was a general favourite. . . .

Henry Craik received the news of Urquhart's death on 28 January. In his diary he wrote of nothing else for a fortnight. It was the severest loss he had experienced, and he confessed, 'I was unreasonably and sinfully attached to him; and often in perfect sincerity, have I felt that I could die for him.' This was a deeply personal reaction from a close friend, but John Tod Brown, a founder in 1825 of the Edinburgh University Missionary Association, probably spoke for many students when he wrote to Chalmers, 'We have all received a most impressive summons to viligance at our several posts in the fate of John Urquhart.'

Among those students whose destiny was shaped by Urquhart's death was his earliest friend, Alexander Duff. At the end of the 1826/27 session he returned home to Moulin, there to delight his adoring parents with the annual copious report on university activities. He usually spoke first of Urquhart, much to the satisfaction of his father who had been fascinated by foreign missions for many years. The story is told that on this occasion Duff made no mention of Urquhart, until prompted by his father's impatient question, 'But what of your friend Urquhart?' 'Urquhart is no more,' Duff announced. He paused and then added, 'What if your son should take up his cloak? You approved the motive that directed the choice of Urquhart; you commended his high purpose – the cloak is taken up.' Duff was not so much asking for his parents' permission as making a statement of his intention to become a missionary. In arriving at this decision he had consulted no-one. He believed he could not even consider his parents' wishes because he would thus risk contravening what he called 'the grand utterance' of Christ, 'If any man love father or mother more than Me he is not worthy of Me'. His parents were first awed into silence, and then overwhelmed with emotion, but they never opposed his determination.

A fortnight after Urquhart's death, William Tait wrote to Chalmers suggesting that he compile a biography of Urquhart as 'a memorial of such unequalled worth'. Four days later William Orme made the same proposal, but he offered to write the memoir should Chalmers decline. The task fell to Orme who was inundated with Urquhart's letters and essays. He virtually reproduced these in full so that the biography of this eighteen-year-old was originally published in two volumes. Through it Urquhart continued to speak to his generation. Adam recorded tersely in his diary for 3 June 1827:

Received Life of beloved Urquhart, much affected in perusing it, uppermost in my thoughts for several days, prayed that it might be useful; considered responsibility of being permitted to form friendship with one so ripe for heaven.

Another of the St. Andrews Six, William Sinclair Mackay, testified to the impact of Urquhart and the Memoir, in a fond reminiscence written in 1860, by which time history had vindicated the belief that Urquhart had not died in vain:

One name . . . rises before me, fresh and fragrant with the dew of holiness. John Urquhart was a Missionary in purpose, first and before us all. The Lord showed him to us, and then took him up to his own paradise. To the eyes of many the half-opened rose-bud is lovelier than the full-blown flower; and his early death gave his word a charm and a power, which a longer life might have failed to impart. Something drew me towards him from the moment when I first looked upon his keen, delicate, intellectual features. Little did I foresee what influence he was to have on my future life. The reading of his memoirs at Exeter, thirty-three years ago, first brought the claims of the Heathen before me with painful clearness. That very night I resolved to be a Missionary: and, thanks be to God, from that resolution I never swerved. It was the happy turning-point of my life.

'How greatly is the pain of parting mitigated, when there is the prospect of again meeting in heaven! Could we hope for this with all our beloved friends, how short would the time then appear! A union for eternity only intermitted for a few moments of time.'

JOHN ADAM (12 February 1828)

Robert Nesbit

11

Separated in this Life

One more implication of the missionary call remained to be faced by Urquhart's friends; the necessity of leaving home and family. Probably this was the hardest obstacle of all. It was not that their parents were lacking in devotion – in fact, with that holy violence which seeks to take the Kingdom of God by force, they had prayed for the eternal security of their sons. Their faith, however, usually proved unequal to the news that their sons were determined to obey the missionary call.

No parent ever opposed a son's missionary ambition as inveterately as the mother of Robert Nesbit. His determination, notwithstanding, to obey the call had been a comfort to Urquhart in his dying months. Nesbit's course must now be traced from the time he left St. Andrews at the end of the 1824/25 session until his departure for India six months after Urquhart's death.

In the summer and autumn of 1825, when Urquhart and Adam were surveying the missionary scene in London, Nesbit was tutor in a Caithness family and also taught sixty-five children in a Gaelic Sunday school. He clashed with his employer, Major Mackay, who insisted on allowing his children to play 'innocently' on the Sabbath. Nesbit, always scrupulous, doubted if he could overlook this and asked Chalmers to find him another position. He characterised the Major as 'a man of those habits and opinions which generally prevail among soldiers, being haughty, reserved, unyielding, tolerating and professing a little religion, but utterly abhorring too much of it'. The Sabbath School increased in size, but his usefulness there was limited since he knew no Gaelic and his pupils no English.

That Nesbit was unhappy is also plain from his diary which reveals deep self-scrutiny and self-loathing. On 7 October 1825 he wrote:

[97]

At this moment my heart is exceedingly hard; and I care not for death, or judgment, or eternity. And no wonder! I have been thinking for above half-an-hour about delivering capital sermons at St. Andrews before the Students, and about the good I shall do, and the instruction I shall afford, and perhaps, more than all, about the admiration I shall win.

These imaginary sermons were not on the subject of missions. Though a founder of the student missionary society, Nesbit was at first little attracted to the prospect of personal engagement in the work. His constitution, he told those who confronted him with the challenge, was not strong enough.

At the end of November 1825 he travelled to Exeter in Devon to take up another position as tutor in the family of Anthony Norris Groves. Groves was an ardent supporter of missions and himself destined for a remarkable career as a missionary associated with the Brethren. He needled Nesbit with the proposition that the high Calvinist doctrines of the Church of Scotland paralysed all missionary endeavour. Nesbit, not to be provoked, was unyielding. But he was protesting too much against a consistent call to foreign missions and, under the strain, fell into 'sore spiritual depression'.

On 30 December 1825, shrouded in his customary gloom, he took a walk in Groves' garden. He was suddenly seized with the thought that he might yet become a missionary. He told himself:

The thing is as clear as the light of day. The exertions and sufferings of a missionary cannot make me more uncomfortable than I am; nay, I trust that God will so bless them as to render them the means of promoting my peace, and comfort, and joy. I cannot now accept a Scottish Church without the idea continually haunting me that I ought to be elsewhere. The thought is from the Lord, and I shall go drooping and creeping all my life unless I yield to it and indulge it. I am sure I should be right in going out as a missionary. I am not sure I should be right in staying at home. Let me feel myself in the path of duty, and then shall I feel underneath me, the everlasting arms.

This great discovery had to be shared. He wrote immediately to the St. Andrews students stirring them up to their duty which was now blindingly obvious to him. He delayed breaking the news to his parents, however, and then pleaded with John Wilson, an Edinburgh student and his future co-worker, to perform that unsavoury task for him. At first sight this appears cowardly of Nesbit, but it was more reasonable than cowardly, because Wilson was experienced in this area. A year earlier, Wilson had informed his parents of his own resolve to work in India with the Scottish Missionary Society, the effects of which are best told in his own words:

And oh! What a burst of affection did I witness from my dear mother. Never will I forget what occurred this evening. She told me that at present she thought the trial of parting with me, if I should leave her, would be more hard to bear than my death. When I saw her in her tears I cried unto God that he would send comfort to her mind, and that he would make this affair issue in his glory and our good. I entreated my mother to leave the matter to the Lord's disposal; and I told her that I would not think of leaving her if the Lord should not make my way plain for me, but that at present I thought it my duty to offer my services to the Society. She then embraced me and seemed more calm. My father said little to us on the subject, but seemed to be in deep thought. In the course of the evening the words 'he that saveth his life shall lose it', and 'he that loveth father or mother more than me is not worthy of me', came home to my mind, and kept me from making any promise of drawing back in my resolutions to preach the Gospel, by the grace of God, to the heathen world. O Lord, do Thou, who hast the hearts of all men in Thy hands, and who turnest them according to Thy pleasure, grant that my parents, with faith in Thy word and promises, may joyfully commit me in all things to Thy disposal, and may I willingly obey Thy will in all things, for Christ's sake, Amen.

Wilson's skilled advocacy of Nesbit's case failed to have the desired effect, and Nesbit's mother raised every objection she could, ranging from the heavy-handed to the ingenious. He would make a poor missionary, she advised, because he was a hopeless preacher, and he would find Indian servants quite impossible. Nesbit sighed and resolved to win her concurrence by 'slow and gentle measures'. Meanwhile Urquhart wrote frequently to assure him that the Lord would open a way.

In July 1826 Nesbit applied to the Scottish Missionary Society without his family's acquiescence. He was accepted and on 15 December that year ordained to the ministry and set apart as a missionary to India by the St. Andrews Presbytery. The next day he enjoyed another long-remembered experience, when Chalmers invited him to tea followed by what the Doctor described in his diary as a 'congenial walk' across the golf links.

On 22 December Nesbit delivered his farewell address to the student missionary society on the text 2 Corinthians 1·3–7:

It appears . . . that there is an inseparable connection between abounding *labours and sufferings* in the cause of Christ and abounding *consolations*. . . . Enter upon the labours of the apostle, and you will enter into the possession of his joys. . . . How know you that God is not frowning on you because you have rejected his counsels? . . . You may go on crouching and creeping through life, without ever daring to lift up your head, or to raise your eyes with confidence to him that sitteth on the throne, because, instead of being irradiated by the light and smile of his countenance, it is. to your apprehension, only enveloped in clouds and darkness. . . . Enter upon the missionary work and you will escape . . . all this misery.

Nesbit dreaded his last visit to his family in Berwick, but the contest of wills was even worse than he had feared. He was forced by ill-health to stay four months longer than originally intended, and his parents seized the opportunity to work on him. He was distressed by the conflict in his own mind. On the one hand his attachment to his 'good, sweet, tender-hearted, kind, and prudent mother' (as he described her in his diary) was deep. Yet he could not help feeling the less of her because her unrelenting opposition betrayed a lower level of faith than she professed.

The son prevailed, and early in May 1827 he left Berwick with the prayer that God would especially support his mother. 'There is one who is better to her than seven sons,' he wrote to his father. 'If she had lost me, she cannot lose Him. But she has not lost me; if I believe in the Lord Jesus Christ, I cannot be lost either to her, or to my country, or to the church of God.' And, waiting for his passage to India, he experienced for 'many days together' the great happiness of those who have forsaken all for Christ.

But the vision of his sorrowing mother returned to torment him. The *Katherine Stuart Forbes* sailed from Portsmouth on 4 June 1827, and, on that very night, Nesbit had a dream. His mother appeared to him, sick and gaunt. She cast on her son a look of reproach as if he had occasioned all her distress. But Nesbit's faith was deep, penetrating his subconscious mind, there to wrestle with unjustified guilt. Not even in his dream did Nesbit reproach himself, but after looking on his mother with pity and great affection, he took her in his arms and said, 'Mother, your *soul* will be saved.'

Nesbit's struggle with his mother helps us to understand why he avoided marriage before leaving for India. Since women were a distraction, he said, the missionary should remain single. Furthermore, to seek the sympathy of another in marriage seemed to him lack of faith. Thirteen years later when he married Hay Bayne, thus attaining undreamed of happiness, he wrote in verse about his earlier attitude:

> My soul appeared to soar beyond the earth,
> And earth's dependencies, – Heaven's love was felt,
> And I could draw direct from thence, and feel
> No want. The earthly channels to convey
> The heavenly fountain's waters to the soul
> I needed not, – alas! I knew not then
> My heart's necessities.

John Adam, the second of the St. Andrews Six to sail for India, met with some parental resistance as he had mentioned to Urquhart, but his domestic situation was different. He was one of ten children, all of whom had survived, and it did not seem unreasonable to suggest, as Adam did, that his parents could allow one to become a missionary. Adam was emotionally demonstrative, and he once revealed at St. Andrews that he never read a letter from his mother without tears. It was every bit as difficult for him to leave her as it was for her to let him go.

Unlike Urquhart and Nesbit, Adam had always been entirely open with his parents about his missionary intentions. As early as December 1825 he wrote to his father informing him of his research with Urquhart into the question of missionary engagement, inviting responses from both parents. His mother must have had reservations because on 9 March 1826, the day before he announced his decision to the student missionary society, he wrote to her giving the interesting undertaking to engage initially for a limited term only. This was first fixed at ten years, but following further negotiations with his father, he reduced this to seven. The London Missionary Society Directors were glad to accept this offer from such a talented and well-trained applicant. Most of them had read their Secretary's biography of Urquhart and were moved by Adam's reference to Urquhart in his application:

My brother, young in years, yet safe for Heaven, has been snatched from my side. We had fondly hoped we should have been permitted to labour together, but this God has seen fit to frustrate: *he* has 'entered into rest' and I would say 'Thy will be done'. May the holy influence of such a friendship, and so bright an example, follow me to my life's end.

After a year's training in London, Adam was ordained on 26 March 1827 by William Orme and Dr. Pye Smith, the pastor of his youth. Adam described the experience as 'the most important season of my life'. As was customary he read out a carefully prepared confession of faith which, in addition to the usual precise definitions of the Trinity, the Word of God, the work of the Spirit, and the nature of man and the church, contained a powerful statement on mission:

I believe in the ultimate spread of the Gospel over the whole earth; that its victories shall be universal, that infidelity and false religion shall give away before it, that iniquity shall hide its head, that at the name of Jesus every knee shall bow, and every tongue confess, and that He shall reign for ever and ever.

On 15 April 1828 Adam sailed for Calcutta. The scene of his departure was 'overwhelming'. For his own part Adam felt very 'physical' and 'too well', words he used to convey a feeling of unreality. The years of anticipation and preparation were over. His father was calm, but the other members of the family were awash with tears as they took turns to embrace him for the last time. His mother had a parting text for him, 'As one whom his mother comforteth, so will I comfort you' (Isaiah 66:13). Like Nesbit, Adam did not seek the comfort of a wife. There is no evidence that the idea even crossed his mind. Twice only does his diary mention conversations with eligible females: one was on a coach, and he hoped it might do her some good; the other was with a 'lady', who unfortunately was disposed to trifle. He never married.

Although Alexander Duff is reputed to have made a declaration of his missionary intentions to his parents in 1827, he refused to consider any concrete proposition until he completed his course at St. Andrews at the end of the 1828/29 session. Ever since 1825 Dr. Inglis had been looking for an agent to head the Church of Scotland's educational mission to Bengal. During the 1827/28 session, Robert Haldane, Principal of the Divinity College, placed Inglis' proposal before Duff, perceiving that his combination of zeal and talent marked him out as the right man. Duff declined the offer, but when it was repeated at the end of the next session, he accepted it without seeking any 'human consultation or advice'. Then he went home to Moulin to explain his decision to his parents.

For two years, since told of Urquhart's death, they had been expecting such news, and they had allowed to vanish the fond hope of seeing their brilliant son settled in a Highland parish. Duff later wrote to his father expressing both his gratitude and his ambition:

Pray with redoubled earnestness that I may be strengthened with all might in the inner man, and with all grace and all divine knowledge, that I may be enabled to approve myself a good and valiant soldier of the Cross, and not merely a common soldier but a champion . . . Will you be a loser by so giving me up to the Lord, and so praising Him for His goodness in having called me to so mighty a work? No, God will bless you with the blessing of Abraham, will enrich you with his faith, and will reward you a thousand-fold for your willing resignation and cheerful readiness in obeying God's command.

Only then did he write to Chalmers. 'The present enquiry,' he explained, 'rested almost solely between myself and my Maker.' He then quite forgot that he was writing a letter and launched into a sermon, always his favourite vehicle of expression:

The work is most arduous, but is of God, and must prosper; many sacrifices painful to 'flesh and blood' must be made, but not any correspondent to the glory of winning souls for Christ. With the thought of this glory I feel myself almost transported with joy; everything else appears to fall out of view as vain and insignificant. The kings and great men of the earth have reared the sculptured monument and the lofty pyramid with the vain hope of transmitting their names with reverence to succeeding generations; and yet the sculptured monument and the lofty pyramid do crumble into decay, and must finally be burnt up in the general wreck of dissolving nature; but he who has been the means of subduing one soul to the Cross of Christ hath reared a far more enduring monument – a monument that will outlast all time, and survive the widespread ruins of ten thousand worlds. . . .

On 16 March 1829 Duff called on Chalmers in Edinburgh where, the previous year, he had been appointed to the Chair of Divinity. Four days later Chalmers attended a meeting of the missions committee of the Church of Scotland to consider Duff's appointment. The outcome was announced to the General Assembly in May: that after much prayer and searching the committee had procured the services of one highly talented academically 'as would do honour to any station in the Church' and endowed with prudence and discretion as well as such zeal 'as to make him think lightly of all the advantages which he foregoes in leaving his native land'. Duff was ordained in St. George's, Edinburgh, on 12 August

1829, Chalmers officiating, and sailed for Calcutta on 14 October.

Unlike Nesbit and Adam, Duff took a wife. This was a remarkable achievement since he had given no thought to marriage until after accepting his missionary call. He had been studying too hard before then even to let the idea cross his mind, as he explained to an old Blairgowrie friend, Patrick Lawson. The patriarch replied:

Well ... my advice to you is, be quietly on the look-out; and if, in God's providence, you make the acquaintance of one of the daughters of Zion, traversing, like yourself, the wilderness of this world, her face set thitherward, get into friendly converse with her. If you find that in mind, in heart, in temper and disposition, you congenialise, and if God puts it into her heart to be willing to forsake father and mother and cast in her lot with you, regard it as a token from the God of providence that you should use the proper means to secure her Christian society.

Himself a master of circumlocution, Duff grasped the meaning of this, and on 9 July 1827 he married Anne Scott Drysdale. They 'congenialised' for almost forty years until her death.

The fourth St. Andrews student to become a missionary was William Sinclair Mackay. Through Chalmers' patronage he secured, like Nesbit and Craik, a tutor's position near Exeter, and it was while there that he read Orme's biography of Urquhart in a day and resolved that very night to become a missionary. A year later he was invited by Joshua Marshman of the Baptist Mission in Bengal to assist in translation work and teaching. He was attracted to the offer because he thought, with his linguistic ability and weak voice, which handicapped his preaching, that he was better suited to such work than the home ministry. This came to nothing, but he continued to nurse his desire until in 1830 he contemplated offering himself to the Scottish Missionary Society. Chalmers suggested, however, that instead he should join Duff in the Church mission at Calcutta. He jumped at the proposal, was ordained in May 1831, and sailed for India the following month.

The last of the St. Andrews Six, David Ewart, was the same age as Duff. He seems to have filled the void in Duff's life left by Urquhart's death. He could hardly remain immune from Duff's infectious enthusiasm as the latter prepared for his departure in 1829, particularly when he received in July one of Duff's most effusive letters. In this letter Duff first depicted his future work in the 'most fearful magnitude' and then swept aside all objections 'in the glow of a feeling which is not natural to flesh and blood'. Ewart's spiritual life was relatively late in developing: it began to ripen while he was a Divinity student and blossomed in a Christian family where he was employed as a tutor after leaving St. Andrews in 1829. In 1834 he was asked to fill the third master's position in the Church of Scotland's seminary in Calcutta. Mindful that Duff was first master and Mackay second, Ewart closed with the offer immediately. He was ordained on 10 July 1834 and arrived in Calcutta before the year was out.

'*It was not so much his words, as the virtue that went out of him, that turned our hearts to the heathen.*'

12

The 'Six' in India

In India Adam's mind frequently reverted to Urquhart. As he walked the streets of Calcutta he recalled that Urquhart had once spoken of 'the living solitude of a city of idolaters', and he could not but regret that 'the lad' was not there to share his labours. He consoled himself with the thought that Urquhart's consecration to the missionary cause might find its fulfilment in others. He had not long to wait. Alexander Duff arrived in Calcutta in 27 May 1830. He had survived two shipwrecks, and Adam was among the first to greet him. That night Adam was so excited that he was unable to sleep, elated with the thought that Urquhart 'though dead yet speaketh'.

Thomas Chalmers also continued to speak through his apostles in India. For the Doctor the grand instrument of Christianisation was the Gospel preached and applied to the conscience. Adam realised that this could not be achieved without a knowledge of the local language. After five months' intense language study he attempted his first sermon in Bengali. Thereafter for him 'great and systematic exertion' was to take the form of constant preaching, ignoring the heat of Calcutta while other Europeans lay prostrate with exhaustion – just as he had braved the snows of St. Andrews while others huddled round the fire. And just as at St. Andrews he spent many hours with Urquhart and Duff in the meticulous study of the truth and original languages of the Scriptures, so in Calcutta he joined with the Baptists in revising the Bengali New Testament.

Adam died, perhaps of sun-stroke, on 21 April 1831, 'A blossom no sooner blown than blasted'. Ironically, the medical profession attempted to save him with treatment identical to that received by Urquhart. And we may suppose that, at the end, he was also not far behind his old friend in that spirituality of mind which he prized so highly. One of his colleagues wrote, 'His whole career in India was a very remarkable one, something like Milton's March of Angels – "High above the ground".'

Chalmers spoke most clearly, however, through Duff. For Chalmers the Gospel was the divine instrument for the renovation of the entire world. But he well understood that those who shared this vision might feel desperation, not elation, when confronted with the reality of the contest between light and darkness. In India, with its hundreds of millions of lost souls, the risk of despair was acute. Chalmers saw that, in addition to a comprehensive vision, each labourer must have a clearly defined and strictly limited area of labour. Comprehensiveness of vision combined with particularity of responsibility was a sound principle both to promote careful evaluation of aims and to guard against inefficient labour and despair.

Duff applied the principle brilliantly. He arrived in India with only one vague instruction: to open a school anywhere but in Calcutta. He surveyed the educational scene in Bengal and within six weeks formulated the plan which was to give him hope of the eventual conversion of many in India and which would leave an indelible impression on Indian education. He ignored the home committee and opened a school right in the heart of Calcutta. He ignored the advice of missionaries who had laboured in Bengal for decades and, instead of using Bengali as the medium of instruction, he used English.

Unlike some eighteenth-century British scholars, Duff was not at all impressed by Hinduism. He described it as a 'stupendous system of error' which had 'exerted an omnipotency of malignant energy over the intellect and morals of the people'. Yet Duff's aim was not simply to undermine Hinduism. That was already being achieved, he believed, in Government schools by the inculcation of 'useful scientific knowledge', but all that had resulted was secularism productive of atheism and anarchy. Western learning without Christianity, he averred, was a recipe for disaster since 'every unsanctified intellect . . . becomes a tyrant . . . an engine . . . for spreading devastation through the empire of truth and order, godliness and sobriety'. Hence Duff's solution was to offer Indians of high caste a 'Christian' education. By this, he meant an education to the highest level in science, which he understood as 'the record and interpretation of God's visible handiwork', and the constant demonstration of the compatibility of all true knowledge with biblical revelation, since all truth is one. In spite of initial opposition from pupils and their parents the Bible was given an essential place in the daily school curriculum. The conversion to Christianity of high-caste Hindus from whom would 'emanate and diverge the rays of quickening truth' was Duff's primary aim and became known as his 'downward filtration' theory.

The higher education of the highest classes in biblical and Western knowledge through the medium of English was Duff's distinctive missionary strategy, and the extraordinary success of this plan, conceived by a young man of twenty-four within weeks of his arrival in India, belongs to history and made Duff 'the prince of missionaries to India'.

Mackay and Ewart were not to earn the same fame, but they were essential to Duff's success, carrying on the work in the Church of Scotland mission school during Duff's many absences in Britain. During Duff's first furlough, Mackay, acting as Superintendent, reported that he had recently introduced the study of the New Testament to a class who had demanded it for a month: 'Their eagerness to get it was such, that we could not enter the room where they were taught, without being persecuted to give it them.' Mackay was particularly successful with brighter students. He was a man of high culture, a classical scholar and elegant writer. He also achieved a high reputation as an astronomer, using an observatory built on the school roof and equipped with a telescope donated by the son of Dr. Stewart, instrumental so many years earlier in the conversion of Duff's father. Mackay was not physically robust and was faced with death so frequently that it could barely boast to be a novel experience for him. He would only comment after each narrow brush with death, 'My chief regret was that I had done so little for Christ, and given so much of my time to the world.' His health shattered, Mackay retired to Scotland in 1862 and died in 1865.

David Ewart, robust and ruddy, defied the ravages of the Indian climate, taught energetically for six hours daily in the school, and devoted his evenings to an increasing number of enquirers and converts. He was particularly popular with weaker students as his patience was inexhaustible. With Chalmers, Ewart shared the conviction that the Gospel could meet the need of all men. Reporting to the Doctor in 1836, Ewart wrote: 'The truth is assuredly capable of being so manifested as to commend us to the conscience of every man in the sight of God. And the powerful agency of the Spirit of life can surely operate upon the souls of the illiterate as well as the learned.' Though not as accomplished a scholar as Mackay, he was entirely devoted to his work, and was utterly dependable. Attacked by cholera, he was taken off suddenly to his reward in 1860.

Robert Nesbit laboured far away in Bombay Presidency. His mother died in 1830. Her dying affirmation, 'No, nothing is necessary but faith to lay hold of the finished work of Jesus Christ', was in words which Nesbit said he would 'not part with for worlds'.

The dream on board ship as he sailed from Britain, in which he had reassured his grieving mother of her salvation, was fulfilled. All opposition to his missionary career gone, she had died in faith. Nesbit's friend John Wilson of Edinburgh University spoke thus to his fellow students about mothers like Mrs. Nesbit:

Examples are not wanting of Christian mothers, who at one time fought against their sons with tears and embraces, [later] laying aside the weaknesses of their sex, becoming alive to the claims of Christ, buckling on the armour of their sons, and exhorting them to die valiantly under the banner of the Captain of Salvation. Examples are not wanting of parents who refused to bid their sons God speed, when they left their native shores, having been led to thank God for preventing the influences of their selfish entreaties, after they have heard of the blessings which have attended them in foreign climes, and the success with which God has crowned their labours.[1]

In the providence of God, Nesbit's long struggle with his mother, and the struggle which every missionary had with affectionate parents, were to prove strangely useful in India. When Indian children were converted and sought Christian baptism the opposition they usually received from their Hindu mothers was heartrending. They would cling to their children hysterically; they said they would die or kill themselves; they would strike their foreheads with bricks and the blood would flow freely. The natural impulse of missionaries was to shrink from an action which could inflict such mental suffering on relatives. This apparently kindly impulse, however, had to be resisted on two grounds. First, the conscience of the convert, determined to seal his new-found faith in baptism, could not be violated even at a mother's bidding. Second, if it were to become known that female demonstrations could avert

[1] Minute Book of the Edinburgh University Missionary Association, p. 58.

baptisms, Hindu priests would ensure that a plentiful supply of female demonstrators was always on hand. 'In this, as in all other cases,' wrote an experienced missionary in India, 'the path of duty, even when it cannot be trod without exquisite pain, is the path of safety, and no one is warranted to turn from it, at the bidding of expediency, to the right hand or the left.'

In this respect, Bombay was perhaps the hardest part of India for a Christian missionary. Caste was there most rigidly enforced, and it fell to Nesbit to comfort and fortify many Indians who, by accepting Christian baptism, lost caste and all contact with their parents. In fact, Nesbit, who could be prickly in his youth, developed into a pastor with a rare fund of human sympathy. He also developed into a leading Marathi scholar and assisted in the revision of the Marathi New Testament. He died in India in 1855. Duff visited his grave and 'there found a melancholy relief in shedding the sacred tear of friendship'.

Alexander Duff left India for the last time in 1864. He became convener of the Foreign Missions Committee of the Free Church of Scotland and in 1867 first Professor of Missions at New College, Edinburgh. He died in 1878, and Gladstone, recently displaced as British Prime Minister by Disraeli, lamented the loss of 'one of the most eminent' in 'that noble race of the Christian warfare'.

Chalmers in Edinburgh, 1828–47, maintained his interest in missions, though his involvement was never again as close as it had been with the St. Andrews societies in the 1820s when he marked a student generation for life. Many recalled with gratitude how their commitment to the world mission of the Church could be traced to their years together at St. Andrews, to the Doctor's grand design, and to the lad Urquhart and his missionary challenge.

Together the St. Andrews 'Six' gave 141 years' service to the missionary cause. Urquhart had made a wise investment of his eighteen years.

'With a full knowledge of the facts, with a personal knowledge of them for nine years, I declare that all that is good, useful, and healthy in education in Northern India, for the past thirty years, is due to him. . . . In this aspect – and I speak the cold language of fact – Dr. Duff has been a greater benefactor to India than any man I can name.'

A FREE CHURCH ELDER
(18 December 1862)

Epilogue

The Scottish Missionary Movement in India: An Evaluation

By 1857, the year of the Indian Mutiny, over five hundred British Protestant missionaries had served in India, a force supplemented by missionaries from the Continent of Europe and the United States of America. One in every ten of the British Protestant missionaries was Scottish Presbyterian. The Church of Scotland and, after 1843, the Free Church of Scotland, were profoundly influenced by the missionary movement which had developed so vigorously at St. Andrews in the 1820s. As one product of the movement later wrote:

At this time the power of a living scriptural Christianity was everywhere touching the springs of Scottish life, and manifesting its healthful and reviving energy. . . . Expansion, reformation, progress, marked the revival of true religion throughout Scotland . . . and students in the Divinity Halls, inspired with a nobler ambition than that of enjoying the status and the emoluments of 'a minister of a parish', began to make this momentous question a personal concern – Where, and in what way, can I most honour my Redeemer and win souls to Him?[1]

It is, therefore, not surprising that, in addition to the five missionaries to India studied in this book, the Scottish missionary contingent included many whose memory will always stand high in the annals of missionary history.

We have already met John Wilson. He, it will be recalled, broke the news of Robert Nesbit's missionary intentions to his anguished parents. Wilson was a founder of the Edinburgh Association of

[1] John Braidwood, *True Yoke – Fellows in the Mission Field: The Life and Labours of the Rev. John Anderson and the Rev. Robert Johnston*, London, 1862, pp. 19f.

Theological Students in aid of the Diffusion of Christian Knowledge which, though handicapped by its name, achieved for the students of the University of Edinburgh what the Students Missionary Association did at St. Andrews. Before leaving for India, Wilson made a thorough study of missionary history and even wrote a highly acclaimed biography of John Eliot, the remarkable seventeenth-century missionary to the American Indians. Arriving in India in 1829, Wilson 'became at Bombay all that Duff was at Calcutta'. A great linguist, he was preaching inspiring sermons in the Marathi language within six months of his arrival. A distinguished scholar, he was instrumental in the foundation of Bombay University and was its first Vice-Chancellor. Wilson gave four decades of his life to India and in 1869 was appointed Moderator of the Free Church of Scotland.

Another outstanding Scottish missionary to India was John Anderson, a student of Thomas Chalmers at Edinburgh University. He heard the call to India when, at the General Assembly of the Church of Scotland in 1835, Alexander Duff delivered an oration so moving that many wept, 20,000 copies of it were printed, and Marischal College, Aberdeen, awarded him the degree of Doctor of Divinity. Anderson was raised in poverty, his father blind, his face scarred by small-pox, and his constitution weakened by tuberculosis. It was not until he was twenty-one years old that he was able to enter Edinburgh University where he excelled first in classics and then in theology. In offering for the ministry, he preached a 'popular sermon' which enraptured Chalmers. 'It displayed,' reported the Doctor, 'great penetration and insight into character; and, in particular, it was distinguished for great urgency, a wonderful power and closeness of application to the individual conscience, a spirit of great earnestness, high unction, substantial scriptural knowledge, sound theology; and contained all the ingredients fitted for the very highest style of popular eloquence.' His offer to pioneer the work of the Church of Scotland in Madras was accepted eagerly. A Scottish missionary journal for 1836 enthused: 'It may at once be said that Mr. Anderson is every way calculated for the missionary work – of true piety – of fervid zeal – of great devotedness, and of superior talent. He more resembles Dr. Duff than any other man we ever met.' His subsequent achievements in Madras certainly resembled Duff's, and the Madras Christian

College, which he founded, developed into arguably the finest missionary tertiary institution in the country.

Another remarkable missionary attracted to India by Duff's appeal was John Macdonald who, unlike most of his missionary contemporaries, made his mark more as a pastor of an Indian congregation than as a teacher in a missionary school. John's father, the Evangelical Highland leader known as 'the Apostle of the north', was minister of Ferintosh in Easter Ross. No prospective missionary has made higher claims for the essentially missionary character of the church than John Macdonald when, on the eve of his departure for India in 1837, he wrote:

The church of Christ is essentially and constitutionally Evangelistic or Missionary – having been called, formed, and sanctified 'to show forth the praises of the Lord', and to 'hold forth the word of life!' – that her unceasing duty is evangelical aggression, and perpetual extension . . . that the evangelization of the world being the will of her Head, is the law of her being: that this law descends to every member of the body, so that the chief end for which I ought to live towards the world under God, is, the salvation of my perishing fellowmen.

The founders of Scottish missions in Central India at Nagpur, Stephen Hislop, and in Northern India in the Punjab, Thomas Hunter, were men revered for the deep quality of their spirituality. As a student of Geology, Indian languages and customs, Hislop was as modest as he was brilliant: he resolved to devote his life to 'the alliance of missions and science' after concluding that his preaching powers were insufficient to justify his staying in the ministry in Scotland. A year before his departure for India in 1844, he wrote:

When I reflect that nothing but an elevated piety implanted by the Spirit of God will carry a missionary through his arduous labours, I begin to conclude that I should not take even into consideration the question whether in any circumstances I ought to be a missionary. This, however, ought not to be the conclusion. I should rather be stirred up to more earnest prayer for the gift of the Spirit, that I may be *spiritually* fitted at least for any department of the Lord's vineyard.

In Nagpur, Hislop was geologist, anthropologist, educator, and itinerant evangelist. He could preach in Marathi 'with a power and effect which could scarcely have been surpassed' and he also mastered Tamil and Telegu. He founded the excellent college which later bore his name. In 1863 he was accidentally drowned.

On the eve of his departure for India in 1855, Thomas Hunter wrote in a vein similar to Hislop, 'For my own part every day shows with greater force that my standard of spirituality must be very high, and my constant prayer requires to be for heavenly-mindedness.' He served his missionary apprenticeship at the General Assembly's Institution in Bombay and his spiritual impact was so great that seven of his pupils were baptised. He commenced the mission to the Punjab at Sialkot in January 1857. On 9 July 1857, during the Indian Mutiny, he was killed together with his wife and child. Two of the martyr's Bombay converts continued his work in the Punjab.

By the time of the Mutiny, then, Scottish missions were represented in the major areas of India. Duff in the east, Wilson in the west, Anderson in the south, Hislop in the centre, and Hunter in the north were only among the most outstanding of the Scottish missionaries. The interested reader will want to know, however, what impact such a small band of men, however excellent, could make on this vast sub-continent with its two hundred different languages, its Hindu majority and numerous religious minorities each communally self-conscious, and the rigid social stratification imposed by the caste system.

Related questions come to mind: Did the wisdom of the Scottish missionaries match their zeal or was their pro-education policy basically a defective missionary strategy? What impact did the missionary movement have on the conception of the Lord Jesus Christ held by Hindus? How successful were Scottish missionaries in planting and nurturing strong, indigenous churches?

In evaluating the influence of Alexander Duff, caution is required because he was, with William Carey, the most renowned of all nineteenth-century missionaries, and his praise was in all the churches, usually in language as flamboyant as his own. Nevertheless, when due allowance is made for the exaggerations of hero worship, Duff's achievements in the sphere of education were astounding and evoke frank admiration. For a generation, his was the largest and most successful school in India. It left its mark on all missionary colleges opened subsequently. Furthermore, Duff's influence was of decisive importance in the development both of Indian educational policy and of India's university system.

By 1837 the General Assembly's Institution in Calcutta, later known as Duff College, had 700 pupils, making it easily the largest mission school in India. Because of its Christian orientation its enrolments, though always high, fluctuated wildly whenever the cry 'Hinduism in danger' was heard. In 1845 Duff reported on one such uproar:

Such a succession of baptisms, or of application for baptism, within so short a space of time, coupled with the fact that there were scores known to be well disposed towards Christianity, and, to outward appearance, far more likely to embrace it than those who actually came forward, led to the raising of a hue and cry, such as has never before been heard in Calcutta. Anxious parents removed their boys and enrolments fell to 618 from 1,300.

Even so the Institution remained the best attended school in Calcutta. By 1862 attendance stood at 1,723 including 211 girls. By 1872 the five schools of the Bengal Mission of the Free Church of Scotland had 2,967 pupils. Duff intended that the colleges would become nurseries for Christian workers, since he believed Indians, not Europeans, made the best evangelists for India. A list of forty-eight of his educated converts in 1871 included 9 ministers, 10 catechists, 17 professors and higher-grade teachers, 8 government servants of the higher-grade, and 4 assistant surgeons and doctors.

So successful was Duff's College in Calcutta that a large number of missionary colleges were fashioned on it. Among the more important were Wilson College, Bombay, and the Christian College, Madras (both Church of Scotland), Robert Noble College at Masulipatam and St. John's College at Agra (both Church Missionary Society), Almora College (London Missionary Society), Trichinopoly College (Society for the Propagation of the Gospel), and Forman College, Lahore (Northern Presbyterian Church, U.S.A.). Most of these colleges became associated with the newly developing universities of India and, with monotonous regularity, missionary college principals became university vice-chancellors.

Duff's influence also proved decisive at two critical periods in the development of Indian educational policy. In 1835 Bentinck, Governor General of India, issued an *Order* which ensured, as Duff wished, that higher education should be in English rather than in Oriental or vernacular languages. The *Order* declared that 'the great object of the British Government ought to be the promotion of European literature and science among the natives of India; and that all the funds appropriated for the purposes of education would be best employed in English education alone.' Then in 1854 the 'Wood Despatch' was issued in London establishing a university in each of the Indian presidencies and introducing the 'grant-in-aid' system by which public money was given to assist missionary and other non-governmental colleges which provided education to an approved standard. In the British Parliament it was said that 'work like Duff's made Bengal ripe for a University', and the grant-in-aid system was a personal victory for Duff who, on leave in Britain, had argued strongly for it before a committee of the House of Lords. The Wood Despatch heralded the greatest period of expansion in the history of missionary education in India. 'Great opportunities were seized by great men, and Christian influence in higher education was at its height.'[1]

Turning to an evaluation of the wisdom of Scottish missionary education policy, there are two fundamental questions on which Duff's contemporaries were sharply divided. First, how wise was Duff's educational philosophy? Second, how wise was the Scottish emphasis on education at the expense of more direct methods of evangelisation, such as itinerant preaching?

Duff's approach, it will be recalled, was to offer to boys of high caste a curriculum in the English language including Western science, literature, philosophy, and the Bible. His philosophy of education was based on the theological premise that the God of revelation is one with the God of Nature and that all truth is one, a favourite emphasis of Thomas Chalmers. Duff's chief critic was J. C. Marshman of the Baptist Mission at Serampore. His zeal for the Gospel was as great as Duff's and his vision as broad, for he was heir to William Carey's great dream of carrying the Gospel to the entire world, and that conferences of missionaries from all denominations should be held each decade to co-ordinate plans for reaching all mankind with the Christian message. Marshman argued that Duff was attempting to Europeanise the Indian mind and that he was ignoring the power of the 'internal evidences' of the Christian Faith. On the contrary, declared Marshman, internal evidences

---

[1] P. J. Braisted, *Indian Nationalism and the Christian Colleges*, 1935, p. 81.

are the most powerful weapons of Christian preachers in all circumstances, and with all people. . . . There are chords in every human heart which the gospel strikes with power. Its reference to human sin and divine judgement was vindicated by conscience; its scheme of redemption was worthy of a holy and loving God, and fulfilled the loftiest aspirations of that human spirit which was made after his image.[1]

There can be little doubt that in this dispute, Marshman had the stronger grasp of the implications of Evangelical truth.

Furthermore, one can only admire the reasons the Serampore Baptists gave for preferring to work through the ancient and vernacular languages of India rather than, as Duff insisted, through English. Just as the ancient religions of Greece and Rome had been undermined by the advent of Christianity while Greek and Latin were preserved, so the Baptists hoped to see the eventual demise of Hinduism and the preservation of Sanskrit. 'Their vision was a land, Christian but still essentially Indian, when "the oriental classics shall be cultivated in subservience to divine revelation, and when the splendid imagery of the great national poets shall be employed to elucidate and adorn Christian truth".'[2]

Just as there were those who questioned Duff's educational philosophy in particular, so there were many, particularly in the home churches in Scotland, who questioned the entire emphasis on education in Indian missions. They were gratified by the large number of Indian children enrolled in mission schools, but what they really looked for were converts. This attitude caused a certain frustration on the mission field. Stephen Hislop, for example, whose school at Nāgpur, unlike Duff's, did not result quickly in spectacular conversions of high-caste Hindus, commented that the anti-education attitudes developing at home proceeded 'from impatience for results', and he reaffirmed his conviction that Christian schools were 'preparing the way for a great moral revolution in a future age'. Doubts about the higher education strategy continued to gain ground, however, and in 1889 the Free Church of Scotland resolved to close its college in Poona. This provoked an interesting response from John Small, who had arrived in Poona in 1877 and was himself a highly successful itinerant preacher. He wrote:

[1] M. A. Laird, *Missionaries and Education in Bengal, 1793–1837*, 1972, p. 254.

[2] *ibid.*, p. 235.

Fervent spirits at home . . . understand the gain that consists of converted souls, and not the gains that come short of that. . . . I apprehend we shall never succeed in clearing this up to friends at home. All I shall say at present is this, that as an old missionary, I see a plan being worked out around me here which I believe to be a divine plan. I see divine truth making its way into the heart of society. I see it revolutionising thoughts and life. . . . I meet everywhere the attitude of mind which silently testifies that the victory is with Christ, while the mouth as loudly protests that his cause gains nothing in India.

Another successful itinerant preacher, Dr. J. M. Macphail, summed up the difference between the two methods more neatly, when he said, 'We itinerating missionaries can influence more men, but they [teachers] influence men more.' Macphail said this in the 1890s when Indian Christians were disproportionately represented in the newly emerging Indian Nationalist movement, and when literacy among Christians was four times that of the Indian average.

In this debate it should not be concluded that those who emphasised the educational strategy were less eager than their opponents to win converts. They just believed that higher education in a missionary college was the most effective way to make converts, at least of high caste Hindus. Robert Hunter, brother of Thomas Hunter of the Punjab, wrote a history of the Free Church Mission in India, and chronicled in great detail all the circumstances surrounding Duff's early converts and converts who became important in other missions. Clearly, for high-caste Hindus to be baptised was very costly; they lost caste and their families ejected them. Missionaries suspected that many of their pupils were Christians in heart, but out of fear of their relatives did not request baptism. Christian obedience, however, required converts to be baptised. In encouraging converts to walk this frequently painful path, Robert Hunter was in no doubt of the supremacy of the educational strategy:

From the year 1798, on for a half a century, devoted missionaries had preached in the streets of Chinsurah without apparent effect, whilst an institution was blessed to gain, within little more than a tenth of that time, a whole cluster of important baptisms. The writer strongly holds that no system has been found equal to the institution one for dealing with the *caste hierarchy of the Indian cities*, the chief successes of preaching having been among the outcaste aborigines, whether subdued as the Pariahs, the

Mahars, and the Shannars, or nearly independent, as the Coles and the Santhals.[1]

In 1853 an elder of the Free Church of Scotland and a confessed opponent of Duff's system arrived in India. Nine years later he wrote this emphatic endorsement of the system:

If a system is to be judged of by only such results as can be expressed by statistics, then I assert that the educational system has made more converts from Hinduism properly so called, than the other. If it be judged of by its actual results in the character of the converts, in their influence on heathenism, in their value to the growing but yet future civilisation of the country, and in that impalpable but, to my mind, plain preparation of Hindu society for a national Christianity of its own, like the preparation of the ancient world in the first three centuries, before the secular power became Christian, then I declare that there is no comparison between the value of the educational over the evangelising system. So strongly do I feel on this point, and so much stronger does daily experience make my conviction, that I should wish to see every white educated missionary sent to the Hindus and Mohammedans proper of India a teacher, with the view of raising native preachers and indirectly leavening society, rather than a wayside or even parish preacher, speaking daily to the people in their own tongue. In a word, I consider the principles of Dr. Duff's system almost perfect for Hinduism as it is, and for the building of a native Church of the future.

Hunter and the Free Church elder were probably right in supposing Duff's educational strategy was the most effective for high-caste, urbanised Hindus, but most Indians were of lower or no caste and lived in rural villages, not cities. It is, therefore, not surprising to learn that by the end of the nineteenth century Scottish Presbyterian churches were not nearly so strong numerically as those of the Church of England whose missionaries were more given to working in rural areas in vernacular languages.[2] Nevertheless, though the greatest Scottish missionaries were renowned chiefly as educators, they did organise native churches. Wilson of Bombay, who was instrumental in the conversion of hundreds, established a Presbyterian Church in Bombay in little over a year. By 1848 Duff's

[1] R. Hunter, *History of the Missions of the Free Church of Scotland in India and Africa*, London, 1873, pp. 110f.
[2] K. S. Latourette, *A History of the Expansion of Christianity*, Vol. VI, p. 144.

converts were sufficiently numerous to form a Bengali congregation which continues to this day.

It is, however, difficult to trace the impact of nineteenth-century Scottish missions through to the present day, because Church union has changed the denominational shape of Indian Christianity. In 1904 seven Presbyterian denominations[1] in India joined the All-India Presbyterian Union. In 1907 the Union represented 125 organised congregations, 16,085 communicant members, and 37,514 baptised adherents. In 1924 the United Church of Northern India was formed when the Presbyterians joined the Congregationalists, and in 1947 the Presbyterians and Congregationalists in the South India United Church (formed in 1908) joined the Anglicans and the Methodists to form the Church of South India. Its membership in 1970 exceeded 1·5 million. The Church of North India was formed in 1970 when the United Church of Northern India joined the Anglicans, Baptists, Brethren, Disciples, and Methodists. Its membership in 1970 was just below 600,000. Outside both these united churches, however, are some very large Protestant denominations including the Presbyterian Church in North East India with a membership in 1970 of 324,000, and the Council of Baptist Churches in North East India with a membership of over 1 million. Professing Christians of all persuasions in India in 1970 numbered 14 million or 2·6 per cent of the population.[2]

Though the third largest religion in India, Christianity has yet barely made an impression on the percentage of the population which remains wedded to Hinduism. But, as the words of a Hindu bore witness, the effect of a vibrant Christianity was profound. In 1879 Keshab Chandra Sen, leader of the Hindu reform movement, the Brahmo Samaj, delivered a famous lecture entitled 'India asks, who is Christ?'.

In an amazing testimony to the impact of Christian missionaries, whom he praised for 'subjugating India', he said:

We breathe, think, feel, move in a Christian atmosphere under the influence of Christian education; the whole of mature society is awakened,

---

[1] The United Free Church, the Church of Scotland, the Presbyterian Churches of England, Ireland, U.S.A., and Canada, and the Reformed (Dutch) Church of America.

[2] D. B. Barrett, *World Christian Encyclopaedia*, Oxford, 1982, pp. 370–381.

enlightened, reformed. . . . Our hearts have been touched, conquered, sub-jugated by a superior power and that power is Christ. Christ rules British India, and not the British Government. England has sent us a tremendous moral force, in the life and character of that mighty prophet, to conquer and hold this vast empire. None but Jesus ever deserved this bright, precious diadem – India – and Christ shall have it.

As God draws new generations of students to the service of the gospel, we may expect a yet larger fulfilment of these words.

Certainly the young men who were so used of God to establish a new bridgehead to India still point us to the means by which the gospel may advance afresh. In the words of John MacDonald, writing from Calcutta in 1841, if the church understood the true need of India

then would she rise up and say (and one day she *must* say it), 'There is none can meet this case, save the Holy Ghost.' Then would our committees, assemblies, and halls resound with unceasing cries of supplication, instead of endless speeches and vain resolutions. Then would that Holy Ghost come forth, with converting power, to raise the dead; and in his divine train, riches and men, unbegged by human voice: and then, by the energy of the Spirit, would the Son be glorified, and God, as eternal Lord, become India's chosen Lord.

A Note on Sources

Sources have not been cited fully in this book as it grew out of two doctoral theses, both of which have exhaustive bibliographies.

F. S. Piggin, The Social Background, Motivation, and Training of British Protestant Missionaries to India, Ph.D., University of London, 1974 (soon to be published under the title *Making Evangelical Missionaries* by Marcham Manor Press).

W. J. Roxborogh, Thomas Chalmers and the Mission of the Church with Special Reference to the Rise of the Missionary Movement in Scotland, Ph.D., University of Aberdeen, 1978 (A lecture entitled 'Thomas Chalmers and the Mission of the Church' was published as the *Presbyterian Historical Society Annual Lecture*, Wellington, 1980). Presbyterian Historical Society, Dunedin, 1981.

On Thomas Chalmers, see:

Stewart J. Brown, *Thomas Chalmers and the Godly Commonwealth*, Oxford University Press, 1982.

William Hanna, *Memories of the Life and Writings of Thomas Chalmers*, 4 volumes, Edinburgh and London, 1850–1852.

Letters and Journals of Anne Chalmers, edited by her daughter (Mrs. A. W. Blackie), The Chelsea Publishing Company, 1922.

Hugh Watt, *Thomas Chalmers and the Disruption*, Edinburgh, 1943.

On the members of the St. Andrews Six, see:

R. Hunter, *History of the Missions of the Free Church of Scotland in India and Africa*, London, 1873.

M. A. Laird, *Missionaries and Education in Bengal 1793–1837*, Clarendon Press, Oxford, 1972.

Memoirs of John Adam, Late Missionary at Calcutta, London, 1833 dedicated to Adam's parents by their surviving children.

J. M. Mitchell, *Memoir of the Rev. Robert Nesbit*, London, 1858.

W. Orme, *Memoirs, including Letters, and Select Remains of John Urquhart*, 2 volumes, 1827, second edition, 1869, with a Prefatory Notice and Recommendation by Alexander Duff.

W. Paton, *Alexander Duff: Pioneer of Missionary Education*, London, 1923.

G. Smith, *The Life of Alexander Duff, D.D., LL.D.*, 2 volumes, London, 1879.

On the University of St. Andrews, see:

R. Cant, *The University of St. Andrews*, Edinburgh, 1970.

Duncan Dewar, A Student of St. Andrews 100 Years Ago: His Accounts with a Commentary by P. R. Scott Lang, Glasgow, 1926.

Report Relative to the University and Colleges of St. Andrews, 1830, Minutes and Proceedings.

D. Young, *St. Andrews, Town and Gown, Royal and Ancient*, London, 1969.

The chief manuscript sources on which this book is based are the records of the St. Andrews University Missionary Association, held at the University of St. Andrews, and the unpublished correspondence and diaries of Thomas Chalmers, held at New College, Edinburgh.

Index

Index

Hunter, Robert 120
  Thomas 115, 116

India, missionary work in 46, 64, 99, 101, 107–111
  Scottish missions in 113–123
  Churches (twentieth century) 122

Johnson, Samuel 24, 33
Judson, Mrs. Adoniram 51

Katherine Stuart Forbes (ship) 100
Kentigern (seventh century) 43
Keshab Chandra Sen 122
Killiekrankie Pass 14
Kilmany 2, 5, 6
Knox, John 8, 80

Lahore 117
Lardner, Nathaniel 36
Lawson, Patrick 104
Leland, John 36
London 6, 18
  Missionary Society (1795), 13, 43, 50, 69, 70, 72, 84, 101, 117
Lothian, William 45
Luther, Martin 4

Macdonald, John 115, 123
Mackay, Major 97
Mackay, William Sinclair vi, 9, 10, 21, 59, 62, 94, 104, 106, 109
Macphail, J. M. 120
Madras 84, 86, 114, 117
Malan, César 19, 20, 21, 57, 72
  Salomon 19
Marathi New Testament 111
Marshman, Joshua 46, 104, 118–119
Martyn, Henry 27, 43, 49, 50, 70
Masulipatam 117
Melville, Alexander 61, 72
Milton, John 108
Missionary Call, the 67 et seq.
Moncrieff, William Scott 51, 57, 58, 60, 62

Moravian Missions 51, 72
More, Hannah 36
Morland, Colonel 8, 82, 89, 90
Morrison, Robert 46, 69
Moulin 14, 15, 16, 93, 102
Müller, George 51
Mykelbust, O. G. 76–77

Nagpur 115, 119
Nesbit, Benjamin 17
  Robert vi, 9, 16–18, 21, 24, 29, 34–35, 41, 47, 49, 50, 54, 59, 69, 85, 89, 97–101, 104, 110
Newton, Isaac 33
  John 30, 90
Ninian (fifth century) 43
Noble, Robert (College) 117

'Offering' the Gospel 45
Orme, William 12, 13, 14, 52, 70, 85, 94, 102, 104
Owen, John 13
Oxford University 35

Pascal, Blaise 3
Perth 13, 16, 52, 67, 91
Philosophy in Scottish Universities 35
Piggin, Stuart ix
Plato 29
Poona 119
Practical View of Religious Systems (Wilberforce) 4
Primars 24
Punjab, the 115, 116
Pyt, Henry 19

Reveille (Switzerland) 18, 19
Rintoul, David 60
Roxborogh, John ix

St. Andrews University, its Moderatism 1, 8
  its chief characteristics (about 1820) 7, 8
  St. Salvator's College 17
  St. Mary's College 17
  its red undergraduate gown 24
  its classification of students 24

[129]